Praise for *Wired This Way*

"The creative mind is a hotbed of alchemy, divination, and anxiety. Creatives are often visionaries, capable of exteriorizing the contents of their minds, in song, poetry and other astounding forms. Yet they are often burdened by what they know, by the trappings of immense awareness and feeling. Jessica Carson has taken a journey deep into the creative psyche, mapped its physiological and psychological underpinnings and crafted a book for the ages, a user-manual for the creative mind, and an enlightening guide for those who live in their wake. A must read."
—Jason Silva, Futurist & Former Host of Brain Games

"Every now and then someone comes along and shows you a mirror that reflects your image in a way that had previously been obscured or distorted. I thought I knew myself pretty well—inside and out—until I met Jessica and became familiar with her work. *Wired This Way* should not only be required reading for anyone that aspires to build products in the 21st century, but also for those people who work with them, so that everyone is playing from the same emotional playbook. The insights in this book are relatable and rare. I'm so relieved to finally have a manual that maps the terrain of becoming a better, and more effective, human."
— Chris Messina, Inventor of the Hashtag & Product Designer (formerly Uber, Google)

"If you are an entrepreneur, you MUST read this book if you want to understand yourself and succeed in business. It's now well established that entrepreneurs are a little bit manic, but this is the first book to explain in practical terms how to manage that temperament, offering simple but powerfully effective guidance on how to avoid its pitfalls and exploit its assets. If your business fails, it will most likely be because you made one of the fatal mistakes outlined here. Simply put, you can't afford not to buy this book."
—John Gartner, Ph.D., Author of *The Hypomanic Edge: The Link Between (a Little bit of) Craziness and (a Lot of) in America*

"The essential user's manual for the entrepreneurial spirit, with all its blessings and hardships. I only wish I'd received this profound, comforting guidance when I began my journey—it would have saved me a lot of struggle and heartache!"
—Justin McLeod, Founder & CEO of Hinge

"This book is a true piece of art and one of the most engaging books I've ever read. Carson's ability to demonstrate the complexity of a creator's mind, from a deeply empathetic yet rational perspective, allows capturing the nuance of paradoxical traits that often go hand in hand. This is a book for every creator who tries to understand oneself better—and more importantly, it is a wonderfully compassionate eye-opener for those close to these beautiful minds. Told in vibrant language and based on the author's vast experience with creatives and entrepreneurs, it captures that the very thing that makes them brilliant and successful is often also what makes them more "complex." I wasn't able to put the book down until reading it from cover to cover, it felt like looking at a mesmerizing painting—a pattern of succinct and emerging colors and characters, composed harmoniously to shape a beautiful work of art. Breathtaking."
—Christian Busch, Ph.D., Faculty at New York University & Author of *The Serendipity Mindset*

"If you are a parent, you read *The Secrets of the Baby Whisperer*. If you work with founders, you should read *Wired This Way*. Jessica's research in the field is a gift to the startup community; founders can identify themselves in one or more of the types detailed in the book, and come to finally appreciate their blessed complexity. Founders will find relevant remedies that help them celebrate their strengths while acknowledging their liabilities. For those working with founders, use this playbook to identify a founder's light, and support them with the appropriate tools so they can fulfill their destiny. Thank you Jessica for so many a-ha moments!"
— Osnat Benari, VP Product & Programming for WeWork Labs.

"Entrepreneurs make a huge positive impact on society, and our world needs more of them. They solve problems, create value, and build prosperity in ways that we should all celebrate. But let's face an important truth: **entrepreneurs are human, not superhuman.** In *Wired This Way*, Carson illustrates how their humanity means that, like all of us, entrepreneurs are full of complexities and imperfections. Most importantly, she provides a clear message to any aspiring entrepreneur that IT IS OK TO BE YOU, to recognize and acknowledge all the facets of your humanity, and to bring your whole self to the creative endeavor. Anyone who works with aspiring entrepreneurs should read *Wired This Way* and share its messages broadly. Her message is both convincing and reaffirming, and is a must-read for anyone with an entrepreneurial spirit."

—Jeff Reid, Founding Director and Professor of the Practice, Georgetown University Entrepreneurship Initiative

"*Wired This Way* is part self-exploration, part examination of the creative spirit, and part manifesto. But the sum is even greater than the excellent parts. Carson gently guides her audience to look inwards, and as she does the same, she reveals something deeper: our best creativity comes not from any one trait, but the weighty work of integrating our darkness and our light."
—Allen Gannett, Author of *The Creative Curve*

"Like the products that entrepreneurs create, Carson iterates her way through *Wired This Way* toward a unique formulation of a path to wellness and wholeness for entrepreneurs. Within that context, she helps us to understand that entrepreneurs are not only people, but people who matter."
—Michael A. Freeman MD, Clinical Professor of Psychiatry, UCSF School of Medicine & Mentor, The Entrepreneurship Center at UCSF

"Like a Canterbury Tales of entrepreneurs, you will soon be walking your journey with fellow pilgrims, all real people themselves, including the author herself, who will show you that creativity and disorder go hand in hand, that your extraordinary gifts would not exist without their concomitant liabilities. With Jessica as our river guide, we are reminded that as we shape the outer world, we must remake our inner worlds as well, giving our minds, bodies, and spirits our full attention, and recognizing that it only when those worlds come into alignment that we can reimagine everything about who we are, and who we can be."
—Andy Dunn, Co-Founder of Bonobos & Founder at Red Swan Ventures

"The potent talent that comes with a creator of any kind must be handled with great care and applied intentionally. *Wired This Way* serves as a guide for self-discovery and growth. Each page nurtures the nature of an entrepreneur. Jessica blends her story with science; her words will help, heal, and harness the creative powers within you."
—Kristin Gregory Meek, Founder & CEO of WYLD

"*Wired This Way* is a huge contribution to the world of entrepreneurship. We need to move beyond the one-dimensional caricature of the entrepreneur in the garage busting through walls through sheer force of will, and instead recognize the deep complexity of entrepreneurship and entrepreneurs themselves. Jessica Carson helps us do that with this book. By illuminating the many different ways of being an entrepreneur, Carson makes a powerful contribution by saying implicitly 'you, too, can be a great entrepreneur.' But unlike so many others, this book doesn't fall in the trap of pushing everyone into entrepreneurship or glorifying its every moment. Quite the opposite, Carson highlights the real sacrifices and

struggles of entrepreneurship. In doing so, she and this book point the way to a healthier life as an entrepreneur, as the first step in any worthy personal or professional pursuit is being honest about one's own experience. Kudos to Carson for inspiring that increased self-awareness and understanding in us all."
—Jon Staff, Founder & CEO of Getaway & Author of *How to Get Away: Finding Balance in Our Overworked, Overcrowded, Always-On*

"An incredibly important book for anyone who takes on the difficult work of an entrepreneur. Carson demonstrates that creators do not operate in isolation, and their creations have an impact on the reality we all live in. By elevating the mental health and well-being of creators, we can see ripple effects across global trends and markets for the better. Investing in the well-being of creators has very real social, economic, and ethical implications, and this is a message that should be emphasized in universities, incubators, and institutions responsible for educating the next generation of entrepreneurs."
—Howard W. Buffett, Associate Professor, Columbia University

"Finally, a book on the inner life of entrepreneurs that grapples courageously with all of our complexities. *Wired This Way* combines solid research with Carson's powerful perception and empathy, captured beautifully in its pages. Carson attends to the whole experience of being a creator—not just the photoshopped and edited versions that we too often see in the media. *Wired This Way* is an important contribution to re-capturing the soul of creative work."
—Luke Arthur Burgis, Entrepreneur, Professor at Catholic University & Author of *Wanting: The Hidden World of Desire*

"Today's technological advancements, if developed and deployed correctly by entrepreneurs, have the capacity to change our world for the better. However, in this time of breakneck innovation, we must also ensure that entrepreneurs can succeed—not just professionally, but psychologically—amidst the hustle and bustle of building businesses. *Wired This Way* provides deep insights and a road map for enhancing entrepreneurial success. Through research on the genetics, psychology and neuroscience of entrepreneurs, Carson is converging the components that make up the individual creator. This work is critical for entrepreneurs and anyone who endeavors to support them—educators, executives, investors, philanthropists, policymakers, and the like."
—Harris Eyre MD Ph.D., Brain Health Entrepreneur, Neuroscientist & Innovation Diplomat. Affiliate of Stanford University, Texas Medical Center and The University of Melbourne

"For anyone working through the chaos of bringing new ideas to life, *Wired This Way* offers you this: the strength of your own complexity. Carson's book acts to refreshingly unravel the oft-repeated platitude to 'bring your whole self' to your work. With each chapter, we more deeply understand our manifold parts and how to intelligently wield them for the betterment of our communities, our creations, and ourselves."
—Jessica Straus, Venture Partner at Dundee Venture Capital & Kauffman Fellow

"Jessica's tapestry of creator stories, interwoven with science, psychology and spirituality, provides a unique and much needed perspective on the mental and emotional health challenges faced by those trying to create a new world. Her rare ability to observe others without judgement has revealed to her the variety of masks that creators wear, and in sharing these revelations with the reader, she sheds light on what might lie beneath the masks of others ... and beneath one's own masks too. After reading *Wired This Way*, creators will undoubtedly feel more understood and more empowered by knowing that their vulnerabilities are superpowers in disguise. The way they are wired makes them special ... but not crazy."
— John Stokes, Founding Partner at Real Ventures

"Carson's style of storytelling, weaving intimate human relationships and personal experiences with scientific and spiritual insights, creates a colorful tapestry that is hard to put down. She artfully blends vulnerable personal stories in a way that paints a vivid picture of the entrepreneurial experience and archetypes that enables the reader to understand and integrate this work on a mind, body, and soul level. I felt transported on a journey that left me with a deeper sense of self-understanding and an unexpected but profound self-appreciation - and dare I say love - for my gifts and quirks, my light and dark, as a creator."
— Kelly Ingraham, Intuitive Guide & Wellness Entrepreneur

"Jessica is a fellow traveler, teacher and student of psychology and wellness who weaves together spiritual and scientific principles into an inspiring message. Whether your background is academic or esoteric, you will find resonant ways to bring health and fulfillment into your life and work as a creator. By blending trusted research with intimate stories of creators— including her own story— she has created an endearing, ageless guidebook for the entrepreneurial spirit. And she has an amazing cat."
— Martin Ditto, Founder & CEO of DITTO

"I have the joy of working with tech executives and entrepreneurs to build better products for improving mental health, and have seen that one of the most critical yet under-appreciated contributors to the success of a product or business is the mental health of those creating it. As a

psychiatrist treating executives and entrepreneurs in Silicon Valley, I'm grateful to Jessica Carson for putting together a book that is the psychiatrist's dream come true—clinically robust, empathetic, and actionable. *Wired This Way* should be required reading for every executive and entrepreneur...it's the first book I've seen that will simultaneously transform your product, company culture, and daily life!"
—Nina Vasan, MD, MBA, Director of Brainstorm: The Stanford Lab for Mental Health Innovation, Clinical Assistant Professor of Psychiatry at Stanford University School of Medicine, and Chief Psychiatrist at Silicon Valley Executive Psychiatry

"*Carson says: Calling All Complex Souls.* This book will undoubtedly become CORE reading and an essential part of the self-study process for entrepreneurs and creatives from all walks of life, at all different stages of their developmental and transformational journey. Thanks to Jessica's brave and deeply, urgently, always aspiring, seeking soul, she has managed to share with us hard-earned insights and wisdom acquired through her own ongoing, evolving journey of self-study. I believe in the transformative powers of self-study, and Jessica shines a light on creators by using multiple vantage points and perspectives (psychological, neuroscientific, research-oriented, emotional, spiritual, and mythological)... all within her evolving awareness ... to make clearer the steps in this developmental journey. She shares her story and the stories of others, beautifully capturing the driving life-force of the creator in all their obvious and subtle complexities. Moreover, her creative use of language propels the reader further into the book, getting them more and more excited about where she will take them next. There is an energy fully alive and present in Jessica's voice as a creator—her message is distinctive, palpable, and magnetic. In *Wired This Way*, Jessica takes us into the intellectual realm to provide data to support her ideas, but what really hits home is her embodied level of knowing that the evolving creator can trust. She comforts the reader with her ability to prepare, guide, and lead them to the top of the mountain ... toward greater self-understanding and self-acceptance...when they are ready to get acquainted with all aspects of who they are. I am so moved by this brilliant work of art—an illuminated path and roadmap for the entrepreneur's transformational growth and realization of true creative purpose."
—Paula Christian Kliger, Ph.D., ABPP, board certified clinical psychologist, psychoanalyst, organizational consultant, and author of *Power Your Heart, You Power Your Mind: Self-Study then Build A Bridge to Someone*

Wired This Way

By Jessica Carson

CHIRON PUBLICATIONS • ASHEVILLE, NORTH CAROLINA

www.ChironPublications.com

Cover Image by Anthony Petrillo www.anthonypetrillo.com
Cover Design by Brave UX www.braveux.com
Interior design by Danijela Mijailovic
Printed primarily in the United States of America.

ISBN 978-1-63051-796-0 paperback
ISBN 978-1-63051-797-7 hardcover
ISBN 978-1-63051-798-4 electronic
ISBN 978-1-63051-799-1 limited edition paperback

Library of Congress Cataloging-in-Publication Data

Names: Carson, Jessica, author.
Title: Wired this way : on finding mental, emotional, physical, and spiritual well-being as a creator / Jessica Carson.
Description: Asheville : Chiron Publications, 2020. | Includes bibliographical references. | Summary: "Creators are complexly wired. In their lightest moments, they are passionate, ambitious, intuitive, and possess a host of other bright qualities. But entrepreneurial spirits are often victim of a darker side of their nature: They are particularly prone to mental health issues, stress-related illness, and other vulnerabilities of mind, body, and spirit. The media has breathlessly chronicled the peaks and valleys of today's creators-glorifying their strengths and villianizing their weaknesses-not realizing that the light and dark within entrepreneurs are two sides of the same coin. Wired This Way explores why the mental, emotional, physical, and spiritual distress among creators is not an indication of brokenness, but of a rich inner complexity that's prone to imbalance. A creator's struggles and strengths are one in the same, and the solution doesn't come from without, but from within. Using the wisdom of 10 creator archetypes found within the entrepreneurial spirit-the Curious, Sensitive, Ambitious, Disruptive, Empowered, Fiery, Orderly, Charming, Eager, and Existential Creator-readers will learn how to integrate the light and dark qualities of each archetype for mental, emotional, physical, and spiritual well-being. Rooted in psychology, neuroscience, mindfulness, and ancient wisdom traditions, Wired This Way is a user's manual for self-understanding, self-acceptance, and self-care as an entrepreneurial spirit"~ Provided by publisher.
Identifiers: LCCN 2020006270 (print) | LCCN 2020006271 (ebook) | ISBN 9781630517960 (paperback) | ISBN 9781630517977 (hardcover) | ISBN 9781630517984 (ebook)
Subjects: LCSH: Creative ability in business. | Businesspeople~Psychology.
Classification: LCC HD53 .C393 2020 (print) | LCC HD53 (ebook) | DDC 658.4/094~dc23
LC record available at https://lccn.loc.gov/2020006270
LC ebook record available at https://lccn.loc.gov/2020006271

For more about Jessica and her work,
visit <u>www.jessicacarson.co</u> or scan the QR code below

Summary

Creators are wired complexly. In their lightest moments, they are passionate, ambitious, intuitive, and possess a host of other bright qualities. But entrepreneurial spirits are often victim of a darker side of their nature: they are particularly prone to mental health issues, stress-related illness, and other vulnerabilities of mind, body, and spirit. The media has breathlessly chronicled the peaks and valleys of today's creators—glorifying their strengths and villainizing their weaknesses—not realizing that the light and dark within entrepreneurs are two sides of the same coin. *Wired This Way* explores why the mental, emotional, physical, and spiritual distress among creators is not an indication of brokenness, but of a rich inner complexity that's prone to imbalance. A creator's struggles and strengths are one in the same, and the solution doesn't come from without, but from within. Using the wisdom of 10 creator archetypes found within the entrepreneurial spirit—the Curious, Sensitive, Ambitious, Disruptive, Empowered, Fiery, Orderly, Charming, Courageous, and Existential Creator—readers will learn how to integrate their light and dark qualities for mental, emotional, physical, and spiritual well-being. Rooted in psychology, neuroscience, mindfulness, and ancient wisdom traditions, *Wired This Way* is a user's manual for self-understanding, self-acceptance, and self-care as an entrepreneurial spirit.

About the Author

"The self is a true "complexio oppositorum."
– C.G. Jung

Jessica Carson is currently Georgetown University's first Expert in Residence and the Director of Innovation at a major mental health organization. Previously, she held positions at a startup and venture firm, and was a Research Fellow at the National Institutes of Health. With a background in psychology, neuroscience, startups, venture capital, and mindfulness, she has both a scientific and embodied understanding of the unique wiring of entrepreneurial spirits, and empowers them to develop their capacity for self-study. Jessica lives in Washington, D.C. with her cat, Cleopatra, and is a devoted teacher and practitioner of yoga, meditation, and various energy healing traditions. In her free time, she likes to be in nature, with animals, and around open-hearted people, and enjoys painting with watercolors—even though she's not very good at it.

Acknowledgments

To my mother, who taught me to be a soft creator.
To my father, who taught me to be a strong creator.
To my sister, who taught me to be a playful creator.
To my cat, who taught me that nothing has to be created alone.

I would like to thank my extended family members who are my devoted and unpaid PR team: Lillian & Guy Petrillo, Virginia Raffaele, Guy & Paula Petrillo, and Faith Resignolo. I would like to thank my friends and partners who provided the love, creative tension, and feedback needed to produce this work: Nathaniel Houghton, Kristin Gregory Meek, Christian Busch PhD, Andy Dunn, Allen Gannett, Justin McLeod, Bryan Wish, Lia Metreveli, Vandana Allman, Meredith Balenske, Paul Rabil, Martin Ditto, Brian Van Winkle, Josh Bernstein, Kevin Morgan, Seamus Kraft, Chris Jeffery, Meg Brackett, Swamy Padmanabhan Ramaswamy, Jason Silva, Chris Keller, Chris Messina, Amira El-Gawly, Harris Eyre MD Ph.D., Diego Rodriguez, Jessica Straus, Hank Murphey, Chase Damiano, Monica Alvano, Naren Aryal, Marc Champagne, Cami Wolff, Mike Malloy, Nate Andorsky, Lisa Cuesta, Derek Brown, Cameron Hardesty, Ryan Webb, Audrye Tucker, Alex Espinoza, Willetta Love, Kelly Ingraham, and Hannah Baker. I would like to thank the professional colleagues and bosses who saw something in me before I could see it in myself: Michael A. Freeman MD, John Gartner Ph.D., Jeff Reid, Tanya Carlson, Eric Koester, Beri Meric, Philipp Triebel, Brett Gibson, Dan Mindus, Brian Vahaly, John Stokes, and Vincent Costa Ph.D. I would like to thank the women I so admire for their joyfully irreverent and unapologetically authentic approach to thought-leadership: Elizabeth Gilbert, Glennon Doyle, Brené Brown Ph.D., Esther Perel, Caroline Myss Ph.D., Lisa Lister, Julia Cameron, Judith Orloff MD, Clarissa Pinkola Estés Ph.D., and Oprah Winfrey. I would like to thank the teachers, healers, and guides who held my hand and reflected my magic back to me when I would (so often and so dramatically) forget: Paula Christian Kliger Ph.D., Kath Roberts, Beatrice Pouligny Ph.D., Yael Flusberg, Amanda Rieger Green, and Kristen Cordell. And finally, I would like to thank those who wrote these words with me: Carl Jung (1875-1961), Carl Rogers (1902-1987), Viktor Frankl (1905-1997), Walt Whitman (1819-1892), Ralph Waldo Emerson (1803-1882), Michel Foucault (1926-1984), and my dearest mentor from beyond, William James (1842-1910).

"Now, my dear little girl, you have come to an age when the inward life develops and when some people (and on the whole those who have most of a destiny) find that all is not a bed of roses. Among other things there will be waves of terrible sadness, which last sometimes for days; irritation, insensibility, etc., etc., which taken together form a melancholy. Now, painful as it is, this is sent to us for an enlightenment. It always passes off, and we learn about life from it, and we ought to learn a great many good things if we react on it right."
−William James

Contents

Foreword: Fuel, Fire, or Both?

By Andy Dunn, Co-Founder of Bonobos & Founder of Red Swan Ventures

The relationship between entrepreneurship and inner turmoil is both symbiotic and parasitic. The tension inherent in an entrepreneur's experience is the constructive fuel and the destructive fire of new venture creation. I know because I lived it: I built a company for a decade in the shadow of crippling ups and downs, enabled by those mood states on some days, and nearly destroyed by them on others.

Unrelenting and untreated depression led to long and harmful periods of absenteeism. It also provoked paradoxically helpful periods of introspection, though unfortunately offering no energy with which to implement change. Hypomania became the opposite, a mood state just a little less than crazy that provided the fuel. It was a propellant for the endless cycle of raising venture capital and running out of funds, the nonstop hiring and the all too frequent firing, the creativity to build the brand, the courage to change the industry, and the abrupt evolutions in strategy to convert the fantasy of a startup into the reality of a company that could endure. I became a mercurial leader with a charismatic and inconsistent persistence, and my life turned into an obvious pattern I sought to ignore: self-flagellation and self-loathing on the bad days, self-aggrandizement and self-medication on the hyper days, with self-destructive urges lurking at both extremes.

If only this book had been available then. The hardest part of the shame and stigma of my personal struggles was that it put me in a box of my own making. I felt alone. If only I had known that disorder is a common ingredient in disruption, and that most entrepreneurs are wrestling with something nearly or definitively diagnosable.

As you read this book, you will discover that you are not alone anymore. Like a Canterbury Tales of entrepreneurs, you will soon be walking your journey with fellow pilgrims, all real people themselves, including the author herself, who will show you that creativity and disorder go hand in hand, that your extraordinary gifts would not exist without their concomitant liabilities.

Maybe the goal of the journey is to realize those liabilities are gifts in their own right, and should invite gratitude, inquiry, and respect, rather than pity, shame or anger. It's for each of us to decide how we process our yin and our yang. What follows is a provocation that we do so not just with self-acceptance and self-love, but with curiosity, optimism, vulnerability and transparency. For it is only in seeking our truths, and sharing them in an unvarnished way, that we can get help, and help will be needed if we are going to not just get through this, but thrive.

With Jessica as our river guide, we are reminded that as we shape the outer world, we must remake our inner worlds as well, giving our minds, bodies, and spirits our full attention, and recognizing that it is only when those worlds come into alignment that we can reimagine everything about who we are, and who we can be.

Introduction: Will the Creators Be All Right?

"There is no light without shadow and no psychic wholeness without imperfection. To round itself out, life calls not for perfection but for completeness."
– C.G. Jung

Over the past few years, the halls of coworking spaces and startup hubs have rumbled with a foreboding message. As provocative research on the mental health and well-being of entrepreneurs has infiltrated the mainstream, the entrepreneurial ecosystem has been left to stew on some rather damning statistics: 72% of entrepreneurs self-report a lifetime history of mental health concerns,[28] burnout is disquietingly prevalent,[112] and stress-related illness is a commonly accepted tradeoff for new venture creation.[22] News articles and podcast headings have used terms like *crisis*, *plague*, and *epidemic* to describe the apparent increase in mental health issues, emotional distress, and psychosomatic illness among creators, leaving them to wonder if there's a plague upon all their shared spaces. Other messengers of doom have conveniently synchronized with these findings, including a wave of suicides among notable entrepreneurs and seemingly daily dethronings of badly behaving founders. As if some new contagion has entered the ecosystem in the dark of night, many now assume there's an outbreak that must be contained and sanitized. What started as a whisper has grown into an outright panic: *Will the creators be all right?*

While these alarmist headlines have shed long-overdue light on the topic of entrepreneur mental health and well-being, this overnight sensationalism has done little to lighten the load on the shoulders of creators themselves. To combat this apparent crisis, entrepreneurial workplaces have slapped together meditation rooms and benefit plans with unlimited vacation days, but despite these well-meaning attempts to ease the frenzy, the inflammatory statistics haven't budged. Many creators are now trapped in the gray area between knowledge and solution—they're aware of the issue, but have little insight into why it's happening or how to address it in themselves and others. They're offered mental health days and deep breaths, but are given no answers as to the root of the issue, and, frustratingly and unsurprisingly, nothing changes. Perhaps the only thing scarier than *not* knowing something is *knowing*, but having no solution, and many creators have found themselves wondering: *so... what's wrong with me?*

Wired This Way breaks through the dusty, dated barriers that block creators from a clear understanding of their true nature as entrepreneurial spirits. There is no single contaminant in the ecosystem, nor is there anything wrong with creators as individuals. Instead, those who self-select into entrepreneurial work are inherently complex, and often carry with them an assortment of mental health diagnoses, cognitive idiosyncrasies, physiological vulnerabilities, and other colorful nuances. Far from a damning burden, these complexities of self are fuel for a creator's work—they are adaptive *advantages* in the landscape of new venture creation. An entrepreneur's struggles are born from their strengths, and no part of them is dispensable in the process of making something from nothing. Therefore, this book doesn't focus on a curative conversation, but on a conversation around integrating the *whole* creator. By engaging in practices of self-study, entrepreneurial spirits can begin to merge all of their multitudes—their light *and* their dark— into one healthy, productive, fulfilled whole. They can learn to become more conscious messengers of the creators within their being who want an outlet for expression.

As I became increasingly aware of these distinctive patterns in myself, those around me, and the related research, what emerged was a series of ten archetypes that map onto the experience of creators. Each archetype—the Curious, Sensitive, Ambitious, Disruptive, Empowered, Fiery, Orderly, Charming, Courageous, and Existential Creator—possesses its own personality traits, motivations, light and dark qualities, and practices that bring it into a state of integration. All of these archetypes exist, to some degree or another, in all creators, but certain archetypes may prove more problematic for some individuals. Combining psychology, neuroscience, and genetics research, buttressed by mindfulness techniques and ancient wisdom traditions, this book will illuminate the path of self-study for entrepreneurial spirits, with the goals of self-understanding, self-acceptance, and self-care. I will share my own turbulent journey, as well as the journeys of those I've had the honor of creating alongside, and will demonstrate that creators cannot celebrate their strengths without acknowledging their concomitant liabilities, nor can they shame their weaknesses without dishonoring their greatest gifts.

While some creators may be frustrated that they need to lift a heavier load to carry the full weight of their wholeness, this is the tradeoff for their blessed complexity; after reading this book, I hope they never again resent their complexities and the effort that goes into their maintenance, nor idealize the notion of "normalcy." Creators are not broken, and what they've been missing, if anything, is a user's guide to their complex wiring. They are spectacularly wired this way, and it's time for them to harness *all* that they are to create—to learn that both their light *and* their dark are necessary for creative work. Archetype by archetype, readers will come to see themselves as vessels for creation that must be respected and cared for, and will gather a curated set of tools to cultivate a deeper capacity for mental, emotional, physical, and spiritual well-being. Creators will not accomplish this by fixing themselves, but by harnessing all that they are and channeling it into their work as entrepreneurial spirits.

And, in case the implication was lost, the creators will be all right. In fact, they will thrive.

- **Part I:** The Wiring
  - The first three chapters provide context on the psychological, physiological, genetic, and environmental factors that contribute to a creator's experience of

distress and dis-ease. In these chapters, the case is made that a creator's inner-complexity is a competitive advantage, and that greater well-being can be found through the practice of self-study.

- **Part II:** The Creators
  - ◦ Each of the ten chapters in Part II addresses a different creator archetype found within the entrepreneurial spirit. These archetypes can help creators identify the patterns that are most troublesome for them, and offer practices to integrate their light and dark qualities.

- **Part III:** The Way
  - ◦ The final chapter provides a framework for self-study through self-understanding, self-acceptance, and self-care. It also offers suggestions on how to incorporate these perspectives into the broader ecosystem (investors, universities, accelerators, etc.).

"Be careful, lest in casting out your demon
you exorcise the best thing in you."
– Friedrich Nietzsche

PART I:
The Wiring

"How can I be substantial if I do not cast a shadow?
I must have a dark side also if I am to be whole."
— C.G. Jung

Chapter 1:
Potential in Chaos

The Electric Muse

*"All the variety, all the charm, all the beauty of life
is made up of light and shadow."*
— Leo Tolstoy

When I was around Jason, it was like biting on aluminum foil ... in the *best* way.

I had never known an entrepreneur before, much less dated one, and I wasn't sure I was qualified to handle this new, peculiar breed of beau. Jason was the founder of a then-unknown app, and from my perspective as a neuroscience and psychology researcher, he intrigued me like the most extraordinary kind of specimen. From the moment we met, there was something about Jason's energy that I found undeniably *potent:* he possessed a powerful charge that was palpable to those around him, and when he had a spark of inspiration, he could create something from nothing with wrist-flicking ease. His personality was magnetic, dynamic, energetic, and nothing if not prone to extremes, and he held within himself a cacophony of contradictions—business school graduate, philosopher, troublemaker, yogi, and founder to name a few. Indeed, Jason was rhapsodic in his complexity, and it was almost as if he was intentional about being unconventional. With a personality that was equal parts logical and intuitive, structured and spontaneous, realistic and idealistic, and other dissonant qualities, his persona was as maddening as it was brilliant. While his vexing depths made him a quirky, if not hopelessly eccentric, character, he was at his best when he harmonized all the multitudes within and channeled his energy into creation.

3

Like many entrepreneurs, Jason spent the first few years of his career in a traditional employment role, only to self-eject in favor of the freedom that entrepreneurship offered him. Entrepreneurship allowed Jason to indulge the most extreme aspects of his nature, and never asked him to apologize for the vision and passion that spilled outside the walls of his cubicle. During the time I was with Jason, he raised millions of dollars, moved his team to a sun-drenched office in New York, and bravely iterated his product into one of the fastest growing apps among young people today. Though he was a mighty complicated being, bursting at the seams with nuance and unpredictability, I came to appreciate that his inner richness was his greatest asset. He held within him the intelligence, confidence, and charm of a whole collection of creators, and could artfully shapeshift himself into whatever a situation demanded of him. Whenever he walked into a room, everyone gravitated toward him with an instinctive pull, and there seemed to be no person, problem, or product he found too daunting. While my life in the laboratory consisted of safety, structure, and sameness, his was fueled by risk, unpredictability, and thrill, and I admittedly envied his spirit and spark, not realizing at the time that I, too, possessed many of the qualities I so admired in him.

But after dating for some time, it became clear that Jason's gifts were complemented by equal and opposite challenges. It seemed that his greatest strengths also fueled his deepest struggles, and his accomplishments couldn't be celebrated without a nod to the murkier nature that lingered just below the surface. His open-mindedness created struggles with commitment, passion frequently waded into obsession, disagreeability often left him in a state of judgment, and there were other large and small demons that weighed heavy on his mind, body, and spirit. He experienced the lows of his work just as acutely as the highs, and while his successes were enviable, even he couldn't deny that his blessings were also his burdens. Cresting the peak of euphoric highs as often as he found himself wading into the morass of his own depths, Jason was in a constant battle with his inner complexity, and couldn't seem to reconcile his light and darkness as a creator. Eventually, the chaos became too much to hold, and with an ending to our relationship that was just as frenetic as the start, we decided to part ways, surrendering to the terms of a dear friendship.

Largely inspired and supported by Jason, I decided to quit my respectable job in academia to join a startup, leaving a world-class neuroscience laboratory in favor of ill-defined job descriptions and workplaces with beer kegs in the corners. To be perfectly honest, I wasn't drawn to entrepreneurship because of my love of technology, and even though I spent years working in startups and venture capital, I really didn't care much for pitch decks or financial projections. I was drawn to entrepreneurship because I was attracted to the *energy* of entrepreneurs, and was compelled by the dynamism of the entrepreneurial spirit. I wanted to be around entrepreneurs because of their idiosyncratic personalities and breathtaking depths that seemed to both empower and deplete them. After years of observing, researching, and navigating my own highs and lows, I write this book in deep reverence of the creator's journey and the souls who embark on it, in a humble attempt to help them navigate the enormity of their own experience. I'm forever grateful that Jason was my first case study, however unwitting, and the muse who taught me to appreciate the light *and* dark of the entrepreneurial spirit.

> *"One is fruitful only at the cost of being rich in contradictions."*
> — *Friedrich Nietzsche*

Homo Duplex

> *"The total self of me, being as it were duplex."*
> — *William James*

If there's one consistency among entrepreneurial spirits, it's their spectacular complexity.

Perhaps the first thing I noticed about entrepreneurs is that they're prone to polarities—they're high and low, optimistic and pessimistic, masculine and feminine, logical and creative, energized and exhausted, open-minded and critically-minded, and other poles of experience that seem as though they shouldn't exist within the same being. I've never encountered a population so receptive to the extremes of the human experience, and yet, these extremes seem to be the lifeblood of entrepreneurial success. While the nuanced nature of creators tends to be written off as an idiosyncratic personality quirk, often creating its fair share of frustration, I've found this complexity to be a self-selecting feature of the entrepreneurial spirit: the dimensionality underlying an individual's persona seems to be directly related to their power as a creator, and the depth and disorder of their experience can be harnessed to produce remarkable acts of creation.

Over years of diving into the research, observing creators in their natural habitats, and embodying the life and career of an entrepreneurial spirit myself, I've come to appreciate that the full, rich, and often messy operating system of creators is not something to be fixed, feared, or cured, but rather, is the very source of their creative potential. I've learned that creators cannot deem only *half* of themselves—only the *good* parts—worthy of their work, and still expect to be productive and fulfilled. I've witnessed the distress that occurs when the many voices within a creator are denied an outlet for expression, and learned that their mighty complex wiring requires a special set of self-care instructions. I've also come to realize that when the practice of self-study is undertaken—when entrepreneurs embrace all of their many selves and harness their sensitivities, vulnerabilities, and contradictions as their blessed and necessary gifts—their power as creators regenerates effortlessly. This book is not a testament to the brokenness of entrepreneurial spirits, but is instead a celebration of their rich nuance. It's a user's guide to understanding, accepting, and caring for all of the multitudes—including the light and dark—within the entrepreneurial spirit. It's a manual to the colorful and complex wiring of creators so they can better care for their exquisite systems.

> "Life is not complex. We are complex."
> — Oscar Wilde

Idiosyncratic Inspiration

"We're built of contradictions, all of us. It's those opposing forces that give us strength, like an arch, each block pressing the next."
— Mark Lawrence

It seems that entrepreneurial spirits are not successful *despite* their bursting nuance, but *because* of it. History has shown time and again that there are tremendous gifts within the personality that's prone to polarities, and perhaps the greatest purpose of this polarity is to provide energy for the entrepreneurial spirit—to provide enough *tension* to generate a charge and a spark. When a creator's life is abundant in contrast, contradiction, and challenge, they will inevitably possess a deep well of motivation and inspiration necessary for creative work. It's not a simple soul who has the ability to create something from nothing for a living, and the concentrated power in a roomful of entrepreneurial spirits is a testament to this electricity. In fact, this very phenomenon is what first drew me to entrepreneurship: every time I walked into a pitch meeting or networking event, I was struck by a buzzing sensation that lit up my body with an electrifying power, and it was as if an energy radiated off of them with a contagious force. While it took me a few years to realize why creators possess such potent energy, I've come to understand it using metaphors like electrical wiring: similiar to two ends of a battery or two poles of a magnet, the tension in their experience generates potential energy that can fuel the process of creation.

Quite by definition, the job of a creator is to create something that's never before existed. To do so, they *must* possess multitudes and *must* experience tension—this is the foundation of their potential energy, and the very source of their inspiration, motivation, and productivity. It's no wonder terms like magnetic, electric, and powerful are used to describe entrepreneurial spirits—they are bursting with energetic potential. It seems that a creator's energetic force—their uncanny ability to transform potentiality into actuality— is not born from the simplicity of their experience, but from the complexity. Potential energy is generated by stress, discord, or distance within a system—it is created when the components of a system experience tension and opposition, like when a rubber band is stretched or match is struck. Creation is born from disorder—not order—and over the years of working with creators, I'm certain the same is true for the entrepreneurial spirit: creators *need* complexity and contrast to thrive. It's imperative they contain multitudes, and they're not simple by design.

Interestingly, although the entrepreneurial ecosystem—a term used throughout the book to refer to the interrelated components of entrepreneurship including human capital, markets, policy, finance, culture, and supports[1]—has been a source of public-awe and media-fodder, this interest is rarely directed toward business models or cap tables. Instead, the attention is directed toward the quirky and complex individuals who are drawn to this special kind of work. For reasons that will be explored throughout this book, those individuals who self-select into entrepreneurial work are inherently nuanced, often possessing significant internal or external tension that generates just enough momentum to create something new in the world. The personality that's prone to polarities is a rich source of inspiration, and without this real or perceived tension, entrepreneurs wouldn't have the *oomph* to fully activate their inherent potential. It may be not a nicety but a necessity that creators have messy minds, sensitive bodies, or activated spirits to be successful on the journey of new venture creation. Indeed, any system that's too calm, stable, and orderly will lack the potential energy needed to catalyze the process of creative alchemy.

> *"There is no energy unless there is a tension of opposites."*
> – C.G. Jung

---

[1] Yaribeigi, E., Hosseini, S. J., Lashgarara, F., Mirdamadi, S. M., & Najafabadi, M. O. (2014). Development of entrepreneurship ecosystem. *International Journal of advanced biological and biomedical research*, 2(12), 2905-2908.

Internal Combustions

"When you light a candle, you also cast a shadow."
— *Ursula K. Le Guin*

Chaos, however, isn't always productive. While a falling piano possesses energy, that doesn't mean the energy will be used constructively—and the same is true for the entrepreneurial spirit. Many of the most resplendent strengths within the entrepreneurial spirit are complemented by equal and opposite challenges, and while the tension in a creator's experience can be used as a creative force, it can be just as destructive. In the external world, this destructive energy may take the form of a fire burning out of control, but in the internal world, this often looks like physical, mental, emotional, and spiritual distress. If a creator's proclivity toward the extremes of experience isn't properly managed, it can result in internal combustions that create the most extraordinary personal, relational, and professional upset. When an entrepreneur dishonors their complexity—either wading into their extremes or rejecting one side of their nature—they risk allowing their energetic potential to burn the source: themselves. To further complicate matters, creators engage in highly demanding work within an incredibly nuanced ecosystem, and these combined pressures can quickly deplete their internal reserves.

In particular, there are a few combustive states in which creators frequently find themselves:

> **Dissonance** is the discrepant nature of a creator's experience, like being both logical and creative, optimistic and disagreeable, or resilient and fearful. Not only is there a tremendous amount of inherent contradiction within entrepreneurs, but entrepreneurial work often requires them to present two different faces, like a front of confidence when they're feeling insecure or a façade of energy

when they're exhausted.[2] Over time, these dissonant identities, feelings, and demands can create cognitive dissonance and discrepant self-concepts, resulting in a variety of emotional vulnerabilities[3] and physical illness.[133]

Intensity is the extreme nature of a creator's experience, like a feeling of consuming passion or fierce competitiveness. Entrepreneurial spirits are more prone to intense psychological states, like passion and commitment,[4] and their work often demands concentrated bouts of effort and focus. If not properly managed, these prolonged states of intensity can result in psychological or physiological depletion, often referred to as burnout.[5]

Instability is the fluctuating nature of a creator's experience, like dipping from energized to exhausted or euphoric to dejected. Entrepreneurial spirits are particularly prone to unstable energetic states that are often, though not always, due to conditions like hypomania and bipolar disorder.[13] The instability of their experience can be exacerbated by the combustive nature of entrepreneurial work, often referred to as a rollercoaster with unrelenting highs and lows.[6]

Unpredictability is the erratic and capricious nature of a creator's experience, like navigating rapidly shifting attention, preferences, or mood. Entrepreneurial spirits are novelty-seeking, sensation-seeking, and often distractible,[7]

---

[2] Shepherd, D. A., & Haynie, J. M. (2011). Venture failure, stigma, and impression management: A self verification, self determination view. *Strategic Entrepreneurship Journal*, 5(2), 178-197.
[3] Higgins, E. T. (1987). Self-discrepancy: a theory relating self and affect. *Psychological review*, 94(3), 319.
[4] Liao, J., & Welsch, H. (2004). Entrepreneurial intensity. *Handbook of Entrepreneurial Dynamics*, 186-196.
[5] Shepherd, C. D., Marchisio, G., Morrish, S. C., Deacon, J. H., & Miles, M. P. (2010). Entrepreneurial burnout: Exploring antecedents, dimensions and outcomes. *Journal of research in marketing and entrepreneurship*, 12(1), 71-79.
[6] Clifford, C. (2017). Elon Musk gets personal about his 'terrible lows' and 'unrelenting stress'. Retrieved from https://www.cnbc.com/2017/07/31/elon-musk-is-bipolar-has-terrible-lows-and-unrelenting-stress.html.

and their work requires them to constantly shift attention from one task to another. Over time, these scattered changes in energy, mood, and attention can create a frenzied and inconsistent state of being.

"Nature implants contrary impulses to act on many classes of things, and leaves it to slight alterations in the conditions of the individual case to decide which impulse shall carry the day."
— *William James*

Calling All Complex Souls

"Man is a mystery. It needs to be unraveled, and if you spend your whole life unravelling it, don't say that you've wasted time. I am studying that mystery because I want to be a human being."
— *Fyodor Dostoevsky*

For many years, I wondered *why* entrepreneurs are so inherently complex. With a bookshelf lined with dusty psychology and neuroscience texts, I began to deepen my knowledge of the work of William James, the "father of American psychology," who was no stranger to the complexity of self. Born in 1842, James was one of the most prolific contributors to the field of psychology, and held a myriad of roles as a psychologist, philosopher, spiritualist, and social commentator.[8] James himself suffered from physical, mental, emotional, and spiritual afflictions, and used his work to better understand his own experience.[9] In particular, James had a keen interest in the role of the self, particularly selves that are prone to

---

[7] Nicolaou, N., Shane, S., Adi, G., Mangino, M., & Harris, J. (2011). A polymorphism associated with entrepreneurship: Evidence from dopamine receptor candidate genes. *Small Business Economics, 36*(2), 151-155.

[8] Kallen, H. M. (2019). William James. Retrieved from https://www.britannica.com/biography/William-James.

[9] Maddux, H. (2017). William James and his individual crisis. Department of Languages, Literature & Philosophy Languages, Literature & Philosophy Working Papers.

extremes, discordance, or heterogeneity in their temperament. He focused much of his work on individuals who experience acute highs and lows, light and dark, and constant battles within an ununified self, noting that although these individuals are often the most creative and intelligent among us, bursting with drive and dreams, their greatest difficulties take place within the confines of their own skin.[10] For these complex individuals, life is full of contradictions and discordance—as if there are multiple selves at war within their being—and while this tendency *can* enliven them with incredible potential, they often suffer from physical, mental, emotional, and spiritual distress until they learn to hold their multitudes.

Today's psychologists refer to this phenomenon in less existential language than James, using using terms like "self-complexity" to explain the amount of dimensionality within one's experience. Individuals vary in their levels of self-complexity—the number of different aspects that comprise their existence—and some believe that those who are highest in self-complexity have the greatest capacity for well-being.[11] However, self-complexity can also create a polarized, heterogeneous experience of oneself and the world, leaving one to feel fragmented, unintegrated, and at war within one's own being.[12] There's tremendous distress that can occur when a creator has too many discrepant self-aspects and no pathway for self-understanding, and it's often a confronting realization that the "cure" doesn't come from without, but from *within*. Whether the discrepancy is a gap between a creator's current self and aspirational self, or a tension between two contradictory states of being, they often experience distress and discomfort until those states are reconciled.

---

[10] James, W. (1928). *The varieties of religious experience: a study in human nature*. New York: Longmans, Green.

[11] Linville, P. W. (1987). Self-complexity as a cognitive buffer against stress-related illness and depression. *Journal of Personality and Social Psychology, 52*(4), 663-676.

[12] Rafaeli-Mor, E., & Steinberg, J. (2002). Self-complexity and well-being: A review and research synthesis. *Personality and Social Psychology Review, 6*(1), 31-58.

Despite this potential for discomfort, it nonetheless seems as though complexity may be the very reason certain individuals self-select into entrepreneurial endeavors. James believed that those with greater complexity—labeling these individuals "Twice Born Souls"[10]—often spend much of their time trying to make meaning and order of their lives, and choose careers in which they can literally *create* a better reality for themselves and others. It's reasonable to suggest that the self-actualizing nature of entrepreneurial work may draw in particularly complex spirits, and while previous centuries may have seen an abundance of poets, painters, philosophers, or priests who largely worked in isolation, the creators of the 21st century are largely those with an entrepreneurial spirit: they're the founders, freelancers, startup employees, innovation executives, intrapreneurs, and other types of creative professionals who are drawn to entrepreneurial work because it provides an opportunity to experience a fulfillment, freedom, and actualization not readily found within the confines of cubicles. Indeed, entrepreneurship may be such a complicated ecosystem because it's filled with individuals who embody these colorful, chaotic qualities.

"Some people are born with an inner constitution which is harmonious and well balanced from the outset... Others are oppositely constituted; and are so in degrees which may vary from something so slight as to result in a merely odd or whimsical inconsistency, to a discordancy of which the consequences may be inconvenient in the extreme."
— William James

A Crisis or...?

"He who comprehends the darkness in himself to him the light is near."
— C.G. Jung

I've come to understand that this volatility of self—the stark contrast between the light and dark within the entrepreneurial spirit—is the source of the so-called "wellness crisis" that the ecosystem faces today. Over the past few years, there's been a torrent of headlines lamenting the epidemic of mental health issues, burnout, and stress-related illness among entrepreneurs. With startling statistics and clickbait crisis statements, the collective dialogue has increasingly focused on the notion that something is *wrong* with creators. At a surface level, I can understand where this fear comes from: when I worked in venture capital and startups, I was overwhelmed by the sheer depths of suffering that took place behind closed doors and out of earshot of investors. From existential meltdowns to manic-depressive episodes to seemingly innocent self-medication, there appeared to be a scourge of suffering within coworking spaces and startup hubs. It didn't take long to realize that entrepreneurial spirits carry an unusually heavy weight of physical, mental, emotional, and spiritual tension,[13] and the culture of the entrepreneurial ecosystem has not been created with the complexities of creators in mind. Indeed, when the inherent personalities of creators meet the pressures of entrepreneurship, there's often extraordinary internal and external friction.

While I can't deny that many entrepreneurs are prone to distress—an experience which I played out to an extreme and will share in Chapter 3— this damning notion of brokenness never rang true for me. I don't believe there's anything *wrong* with creators, nor do I accept that they need to be "cured." Instead, it seems that entrepreneurial spirits are individuals of incredible inner richness who often struggle to understand the discrepancy between the light and dark within their being, and this feeling of disunity—this fundamental misunderstanding of the way they're wired—can make them more susceptible to all manner of physical, mental, emotional, and spiritual illness. However, contrary to the messages disseminated by the media, there is no curse, plague, epidemic, or crisis at play. There is no malevolent force at work, nor is there actual agreement among experts that rate of mental illness in the

---

[13] Freeman, M. A., Johnson, S. L., Staudenmaier, P. J., & Zisser, M. R. (2015). Are entrepreneurs "touched with fire". *Unpublished manuscript. San Francisco, CA: University of California San Farancisco. Retrieved from http://www.michaelafreemanmd.com/Research_files/Are%20Entrepreneurs%20Touched%20with%20Fire%20(pre-pub%20n)%204-17-15.pdf.*

general population is increasing.[14] Instead, the shadows within the entrepreneurial spirit now have the opportunity to emerge through increased diagnosis and public awareness, and the time has come for creators to attend to the vessel through which creation takes place: themselves.

"That is creative life. It is made up of divine paradox. To create one must be willing to be stone stupid, to sit upon a throne on top of a jackass and spill rubies from one's mouth. Then the river will flow, then we can stand in the stream of it raining down."
— Clarissa Pinkola Estés

To Cure or Not to Cure

"One does not become enlightened by imagining figures of light, but by making the darkness conscious. The latter procedure, however, is disagreeable and therefore not popular."
— C.G. Jung

This book is not designed to be a prescription or a cure, nor is it a manifesto on darkness or a monologue of chirpy self-help. Instead, it makes the case that those individuals who self-select into entrepreneurship are complex, dynamic, and delightfully contradictory, and inevitably, this means that the entrepreneurial ecosystem will be full of individuals who are prone to distress. But, given that creators thrive on the richness of their inner experience, the solution is not to be found in curing the entrepreneurial spirit; if creators were to fix, shame, or hide the parts of themselves that others perceive as broken, they may very well dilute the essence that makes them so potent. According to James, the goal is not to eliminate, ignore, or shame the many selves within, as this inner tension makes complex individuals *most* capable of achieving renewal and rebirth. Instead, the goal is to undergo a process of

---

[14] Carey, B. (2012). A Tense Compromise on Defining Disorders. Retrieved from https://www.nytimes.com/2012/12/11/health/a-compromise-on-defining-and-diagnosing-mental-disorders.html.

balancing, integration, and unification—to understand that one must leverage every crevice of one's being as a source of creative potential. In James's words, the more "intense and sensitive and subject to diversified temptations" one is, the more one must concentrate on "straightening out and unifying the inner self," and that the process is not merely one of reversion to health, but of awakening to one's fullest self and spirit. While James admits that this process often involves suffering, it's this path that can lead individuals toward a deeper kind of consciousness.

Creators need not silence their complicated spirits into submission, for to do so would be a threat to the vitality and viability of the entrepreneurial ecosystem. Instead, creators must learn to understand and harness their exquisite and often sensitive wiring—they must come to see their fullness as their competitive advantage while learning to mindfully regulate the tension between their light and dark. Only when creators are armed with an awareness of the way they're wired can they consistently and efficiently integrate their inner experience, and straddle the most productive hingepoint of their polarized nature. Through the practice of self-study, creators can activate their inherent capacity for self-regulation, and intuitively guide themselves toward a state of wholeness—a state in which they create harmoniously with all of their many multitudes. That said, creators should expect to find themselves in occasional states of distress over the course of their careers—they haven't chosen a job, they've chosen a hero's journey, and they will inevitably face challenges. It's therefore important to toss out expectations of perfect balance or nirvanic bliss, as this is not what it means to be whole. Instead, wholeness is a natural consequence of gracefully regulating the give and take, ebb and flow, and yin and yang of the human experience. Self-study isn't a one-time cure, but a life's work involving daily, intentional, fiercely curious participation.

It's also important to note that this framework isn't meant to glorify suffering, or glamorize the plight of the "troubled creator" or "mad genius"—complexity and suffering are not *inevitable* bedmates, though they do tend to find each other's company. In this book, it will become clear that a creator's "suffering" may not look or feel like suffering, and may in fact appear to be quite the opposite. For example, a creator who is cresting the highs of mania or hulled up in a fit of impassioned work may be productive and excited, but is nonetheless in an imbalanced state. Distress doesn't only look like depression or disease, and I would hate for creators to think that if they haven't explicitly suffered then they aren't a "real" entrepreneurial spirit. In my opinion, the entrepreneur with a too-disagreeable temper, too-grandiose vision, or too-distractible mind is also experiencing distress; while the entrepreneur in the depths of a depression or midst of an identity crisis may look or feel "lower," both are struggling in their own way. It's important that creators don't assign points to themselves for suffering or lack thereof, but instead realize that these moments of combustion are windows into their greatest strengths, as well as the qualities that are begging for integration.

> "You are imperfect, you are wired for struggle, but you are worthy of love and belonging."
> — Brené Brown

How To Use This Book

> "You wanted to accept everything. So accept madness too. Let the light of your madness shine, and it will suddenly dawn on you. Madness is not to be despised and not to be feared, but instead you should give it life."
> — C.G. Jung

Dear creator,

This book will take you on a journey of the ten creator archetypes within the entrepreneurial spirit to help you better understand the way you're wired. On this journey, you'll be guided to learn about each archetype's light and dark qualities, and will be offered tools and practices that will shepherd you toward greater mental, emotional, physical, and spiritual well-being. Each chapter in Part

Curious Creator: Openness to Experience
Sensitive Creator: Intuition
Ambitious Creator: Achievement Motivation
Disruptive Creator: Disagreeability
Empowered Creator: Ego
Fiery Creator: Passion
Orderly Creator: Conscientiousness
Charming Creator: Charisma
Courageous Creator: Optimism
Existential Creator: Self-Actualization

II addresses a different creator archetype found within the entrepreneurial spirit —the Curious, Sensitive, Ambitious, Disruptive, Empowered, Fiery, Orderly, Charming, Courageous, and Existential Creator—and offers techniques for self-understanding, self-acceptance, and self-care. Archetypes (Greek for original, old, pattern, model or type) are common frameworks used in psychology and philosophy to explore symbolic patterns that reside within the collective, and can be thought of as characters who will help you gain deeper insight into your own thoughts, emotions, and behaviors. Each of these archetypes has its own primary personality theme, motivation, strengths, and weaknesses, and while certain archetypes will resonate with you more than others, *aspects* of each archetype reside within every entrepreneurial spirit. **You may identify with one, several, or all of the archetypes.**

Each chapter on the ten creator archetypes contains a chart with the following information:

- **Dimension** is the research-driven personality feature behind each archetype. Each archetype has a corresponding dimension: Openness to experience, intuition, achievement motivation, disagreeability, ego, passion, conscientiousness, charisma, optimism, and self-actualization. According to research cited throughout the book, each of these dimensions is more prominent in entrepreneurs than non-entrepreneurs, and will therefore have a powerful impact on their work and their well-being.
- **Motivation & Mantra** capture the essence, intention, and driving force of the archetype. They reflect the *why* behind the archetype's work.

- **Tension** is the primary conflict the archetype will face. The tension is each archetype's double-edged sword—it is the blessing and challenge.
- **Light Qualities** are the descriptors of each archetype in its strongest, healthiest, and most productive embodiment.
- **Dark Qualities** are the descriptors of each archetype in weakest, least healthy, and most unproductive embodiment.
- **To Integrate** is the process through which each archetype can find inner-harmony. It is the practice that can make the archetype *whole*. It's the recovery tool that will prevent the tension from depleting the creator.

Using this framework, you will come to realize that the light and dark aspects of your wiring are one in the same. Your strengths and struggles are two sides of the same coin, and you cannot celebrate your brightness and condemn your shadow without losing part of your creative magic. The goal is not to ignore, eliminate, or shame your areas of tension, but to meet them with awareness and acceptance so that you can deepen your capacity for self-regulation. This framework will not guarantee perfect "lightness," but will instead help you identify the most extreme areas of dissonance, intensity, instability, and unpredictability in your experience so you can create with greater ease. For the purpose of absorbing and integrating the learnings, I recommend reading Part II at a pace of one chapter per day for ten days, and even though some chapters will resonate for you more than others, I recommend reading every chapter, as the insights will also help you better understand the experiences of colleagues, co-founders, and employees.

"Peace cannot be reached by the simple addition of pluses and elimination of minuses from life... the normal evolution of character chiefly consist in the straightening out and unifying of the inner self."
— *William James*

My Intention for You

"Wholeness is not achieved by cutting off a portion of one's being,
but by integration of the contraries."
— C.G. Jung

Following in the footsteps of countless creators who have transmuted their challenges into inspiration, this book is a call to channel your potent energy into constructive, not destructive, acts of creation. It will ask you to claim any lost, disjointed, under-exercised, or overused parts of your personality so that you can return to your whole creative self. It will test you to elevate your intentionality as a creator, not by forcing upon you any specific meditation techniques or breathing practices, but by offering manual for self-study, and insisting that you choose only the recommendations that resonate with you. In this process, you will not only become more aware of your own mind, body, and spirit, but will also have a clearer understanding of the impact of your creations on the collective—you will realize that a creation always reflects the health of its creator, and that you have a societal responsibility to elevate the integrity of your own operating system. This book is a guide to your journey as a creator which is, at its essence, a journey of self-study. It's not a journey of fixing yourself, but a journey of identifying your greatest potentialities and sharing them through the act of creation. It's not a journey of becoming more, but a journey of coming back to your most essential self.

Physicists and philosophers are of the same mind when they say that progress doesn't come from *simplification*, but from improving mechanisms to address *complexity*. Reality is woven in opposing truths—a principle that is valid in both physics and psychology—and creative consciousness arises from the ability to hold and harness it all. It's my intention that you finish this book with not only an understanding of your wiring, but with an exuberant pride in your spectacular multitudes. I hope that you will see every quality which you have only ever deemed ugly, shameful, or bad as your blessing. I hope that you will consciously align with all of the creators within your being who want to speak, and come to view your complexity as a gift *and* a responsibility. Please relish in taking up all the space that is you—your highs and lows, your light and dark—so that you can become a clear conduit to create your life's work. By the end of the book, you will realize that your struggles *and* your strengths are your energy source as a creator, and self-study is the mechanism that allows you to harness your powerful wiring without combusting in the process.

In this book, the journey of self-study is as follows:

Self-Understanding: First, you will embark on a journey of self-understanding, which is the primary focus of this book. You will be guided to understand the light and dark within the entrepreneurial spirit. The goal is not to provide you with excessive prescriptions, regimens, or trite recommendations, but rather, to provide you with a mirror through which self-examination can take place. While the purpose of self-understanding isn't *necessarily* to heal, healing is often a side effect of self-understanding.

Self-Acceptance: Next, armed with the tools of self-understanding, you will explore self-acceptance. At this stage, you will have a better understanding of your light and dark, and can identify patterns as they arise, preventing the projection of unresolved inner conflicts onto your creations or those around you. Self-acceptance is a crucial intermediary step between self-understanding and self-care, as it modulates your capacity to engage with yourself and your work with less resistance, fear, or judgement, thereby reducing the likelihood that your temporary struggles will turn into prolonged suffering.

Self-Care: Finally, once you achieve greater self-understanding and self-acceptance, you can engage in sustainable self-care. Many coaches, healers, and wellness centers *start* with self-care which isn't especially helpful, much less sustainable, without the foundation of self-understanding and self-acceptance. Particularly for the entrepreneurial spirit who is wont to do things to extremes, self-care should be practiced mindfully and with utmost self-compassion, lest the self-care process become yet another source of burnout.

Nothing great has ever been created from steadiness and stability alone, and only when you learn to embrace your multitudes can you tap into your full creative and productive potential. In my experience, the most actualized entrepreneurs are those who use their internal chaos as their brilliance, their gift, and their magic. The solution, if I may be so bold, is to honor and express *all* the creators within your being: It's all necessary. It's all valid. It's all you.

"It is as if the opposites of the world, whose contradictoriness and conflict make all our difficulties and troubles, were melted into unity."
— William James

Chapter 2:
Not So Faulty Wiring

Defining the Entrepreneurial Spirit

"If we accept the whole, shall we do so as if stunned into submission...
or shall we do so with enthusiastic assent?"
— *William James*

Researchers have long lamented the challenge of defining entre-preneurs—unsurprisingly, it's quite a complex, amorphous group.[15] Many assume that the title of "entrepreneur" is reserved for venture-backed, Silicon Valley startup founders, but this narrow definition leaves out a rich assortment of entrepreneurial individuals like freelancers, small business owners, innovation professionals, creative strategists, intrapreneurs, startup employees, aspiring entrepreneurs, and the like. In my view, a creator does not need to be a "technologist" nor a prototypical "creative" to be an entre-preneurial spirit, and I use this term to hold space for the individuals who have largely been left out of the literature. For the purpose of this book, entrepreneurial spirits are characterized by their intention rather than their job description, and can be thought of as individuals who turn nothing into something for a living—they use themselves as vehicles for the creative process at scale. That said, in an effort to keep this book rooted in research, the dimensions outlined are based on studies conducted on more classically-defined entrepreneurs. While I have no doubt the material will resonate with creators more broadly, I encourage readers to take what is useful and leave what is not.

---

[15] Cunningham, J. B., & Lischeron, J. (1991). Defining entrepreneurship. *Journal of small business management*, 29(1), 45-61.

"We are the vessels through which energy becomes matter in this life."
— Caroline Myss

A Complicated Foundation

"A man is whole only when he takes into account his shadow."
— Djuna Barnes

To set the stage for the rest of the book, it's important to identify the internal and external variables that contribute to the paradoxical and often combustive nature of creators. While the intent of this chapter isn't to focus on what's *wrong* with entrepreneurial spirits, there are certain undeniable challenges they face from a physiological, psychological, and cultural standpoint. The next few pages will review some of the genetic vulnerabilities, environmental triggers, and psychological predispositions that can amplify a creator's experience of distress and dis-ease: 1. Clinical & Subclinical Mental Health Issues; 2. Emotional & Spiritual Challenges; and 3. Stress-Related Illness.

1. Clinical & Subclinical Mental Health Issues

Perhaps the most commonly discussed challenge among entrepreneurs is their mental health. Research has shown that 72% of entrepreneurs report they are directly or indirectly affected by mental health conditions, compared with 48% of non-entrepreneurs.[13] While mental health diagnoses receive the lion's share of press attention, many entrepreneurs do not have a diagnosable mental health issue, but still experience subclinical manifestations of these conditions. For example, an entrepreneur may not suffer from substance abuse but may experience work addiction,[16] or may

---

[16] Keskin, G., Gümü soy, S., & Aktekin, E. (2015). Entrepreneurship: Is it an addiction?. *Procedia-Social and Behavioral Sciences, 195*, 1694-1697.

not have clinical depression but still experience periods of low mood and energy.

Depression: Thirty percent of entrepreneurs report a lifetime history of depression, which is two times higher than controls.[13] Characterized by low mood and energy, changes in eating, sleeping, social behavior, and more, depression is the most common mental health issue among entrepreneurs.

ADHD: Twenty-nine percent of entrepreneurs report a lifetime history of ADHD, which is almost six times higher than controls.[13] ADHD is characterized by inattention, hyperactivity, difficulty following instructions, and disorganization.

Substance Abuse: Twelve percent of entrepreneurs report a lifetime history of substance abuse, which is three times higher than controls.[13] In addition to substance abuse, entrepreneurs commonly exhibit other behavioral addictions, like addiction to work, commonly referred to as "entrepreneurship addiction."[16]

Bipolar: Eleven percent of entrepreneurs report a lifetime history of bipolar disorder, which is 11 times higher than controls.[13] Characterized by unusual shifts in mood and energy, individuals with bipolar experience periods of energy and elation, followed by periods of low energy and depressive affect.

Hypomania: It's not an unfounded notion that entrepreneurs are largely hypomanic.[17] Often characterized by high energy, hypomania is a mild form of mania that is linked to grandiosity, high self-esteem, distractibility, irritability, risk taking, increase in goal-oriented activity, and decreased need for sleep.[18]

---

[17] Gartner, J. D. (2008). *The hypomanic edge: the link between (a little) craziness and (a lot of) success in America.* Simon and Schuster.

2. Emotional & Spiritual Challenges

Many entrepreneurs experience challenges that are not necessarily clinical in nature, but nonetheless affect their emotional and spiritual well-being. These challenges will be discussed in more detail throughout the book, but a few common examples include:

Imposter Syndrome: A psychological pattern in which an entrepreneur doubts their accomplishments, believes their successes are due to luck, and fears being exposed as a fraud.[19] Surprisingly, this is often seen in the most capable, intelligent, and high-achieving entrepreneurs, and appears to be most common in female entrepreneurs.

Crisis of Meaning: A moment in which when an entrepreneur's sense of meaning, purpose, value, or sense of self is threatened.[20] Anecdotally, this often occurs after a failure, acquisition, change in responsibilities, or another challenging moment in the growth of a company.

Obsessive Passion: A type of passion in which an entrepreneur is compulsively committed to their work, often resulting in burnout.[21] Their attachment to work conflicts with a full, rich life, and they often experience distraction, guilt, and anxiety when they're not engaged with work.

3. Stress-related Illness

In addition to mental, emotional, and spiritual distress, entrepreneurs are more likely to experience stress-related physical health

---

[18] Furnham, Adrian, et al. "Personality, hypomania, intelligence and creativity." *Personality and Individual Differences 44.5* (2008): 1060-1069.

[19] Ladge, J., Eddleston, K. A., & Sugiyama, K. (2019). Am I an entrepreneur? How imposter fears hinder women entrepreneurs' business growth. *Business Horizons*.

[20] James, R. K., & Gilliland, B. E. (2012). *Crisis intervention strategies*. Nelson Education.

[21] Cardon, M. S., Wincent, J., Singh, J., & Drnovsek, M. (2009). The nature and experience of entrepreneurial passion. *Academy of management Review, 34(3)*, 511-532.

outcomes than employees.[22] Stress-related illness is often the body's way of drawing attention to persistent, unresolved issues of the mind and spirit, and stress gone too-long unmanaged can wear down a creator's psychological and physiological resources. Depending on whether an entrepreneur's stresses are acute, like an upcoming pitch, or chronic, like a fear of failure, stress-related illnesses can take on different manifestations. Stress has been clearly shown to have deleterious effects on a myriad of physical health outcomes,[23] and the following represent common complaints among creators:

> **Weakened Immunity:** Intense and/or persistent stress can weaken the body's immune system, making it more susceptible to illness, and slower to heal and recover from injury.[24] If left unaddressed, weakened immunity from stress can eventually result in autoimmune issues.

> **Sleeping Problems:** Many entrepreneurs report stress-related sleeping problems, like insomnia. A condition characterized by chronic difficulty falling or staying asleep, insomnia is often linked to stress, erratic travel and work schedules, and substances like caffeine and alcohol.[25]

> **GI Troubles:** Entrepreneurs frequently self-report gastro-intestinal troubles like heartburn, irritable bowel syndrome, food sensitivities, and more. Research has increasingly clarified the gut-mind connection, and it appears that prolonged stress can trigger the onset of GI disorders.[26]

---

[22] Cardon, M. S., & Patel, P. C. (2015). Is stress worth it? Stress-related health and wealth trade-offs for entrepreneurs. *Applied Psychology, 64*(2), 379-420.

[23] Prottas, D.J., & Thompson, C.A. (2006). Stress, satisfaction, and the work–family interface: A comparison of self-employed business owners, independents, and organizational employees. *Journal of Occupational Health Psychology, 11*(4), 366– 378.

[24] Reed, R. G., & Raison, C. L. (2016). Stress and the immune system. *Environmental influences on the immune system* (pp. 97-126). Springer, Vienna.

[25] "Insomnia." *Mayo Clinic,* Mayo Foundation for Medical Education and Research, 15 Oct. 2016, https://www.mayoclinic.org/diseases-conditions/insomnia/symptoms-causes/syc-20355167.

[26] Mayer, E. A. (2000). The neurobiology of stress and gastrointestinal disease. *Gut, 47*(6), 861-869.

"The truly creative mind in any field is no more than this: A human creature born abnormally, inhumanly sensitive. To him... a touch is a blow, a sound is a noise, a misfortune is a tragedy, a joy is an ecstasy, a friend is a lover, a lover is a god, and failure is death. Add to this cruelly delicate organism the overpowering necessity to create, create, create — so that without the creating of music or poetry or books or buildings or something of meaning, his very breath is cut off from him. He must create, must pour out creation. By some strange, unknown, inward urgency he is not really alive unless he is creating."
— Pearl S. Buck

A Nuanced Dilemma

"Creativity — like human life itself — begins in darkness."
—Julia Cameron

While it's commonly believed that the stressful nature of entre-preneurship is to blame for mental and physical illness in entrepreneurs, the causal relation-ship isn't so simple. There are many variables at play in the manifestation of disharmony and disease, including the: 1. Genetic Predisposition of Entrepreneurs; 2. Nature of Entrepreneurial Work; and 3. Culture of the Entrepreneurial Ecosystem.

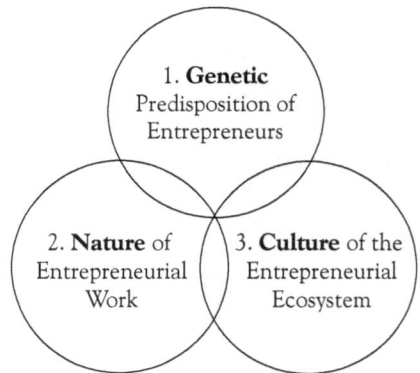

1. **Genetic** Predisposition of Entrepreneurs

2. **Nature** of Entrepreneurial Work

3. **Culture** of the Entrepreneurial Ecosystem

1. Genetic Predisposition of Entrepreneurs

The prevalence of distress among entrepreneurs may not be high simply because of the stresses of entrepreneurial work and the culture of the entrepreneurial ecosystem, but because of the unique wiring of the individuals who self-select into entrepreneurship. According to the attraction-selection-attrition model, individuals should be expected to opt into certain jobs, activities, or environments if they possess inherent attributes that offer them an adaptive advantage in that context.[27] For example, someone with a low risk tolerance might self-select into an administrative role in a large company that offers stability and security, while someone with a high risk tolerance may self-select into an entrepreneurial role that offers dynamism and ambiguity. When examining the types of individuals who self-select into entrepreneurship, it's believed that individuals with certain mental health challenges become entrepreneurs because their challenges actually make them more likely to *succeed* as an entrepreneur.[28] In other words, they're not entrepreneurs *despite* these vulnerabilities, but *because of* these vulnerabilities—their mental health diagnosis provides an adaptive advantage in the entrepreneurial context. While conversations about entrepreneurial well-being can easily feel damning, this perspective offers a remarkable silver lining: some of the most stigmatized qualities among entrepreneurs may also allow them to achieve remarkable success.

> **Depression:** Research has shown that depression is connected with creativity,[29] emotional intelligence,[30] cognitive intelligence,[31] focused thinking,[32] and more. From an evolutionary perspective, researchers believe depression may be an adaptive state that allows an individual to conserve energy, mindfully engage with their environment, and focus on the problem at hand.[32] For entrepreneurs, this tendency may allow them to solve complex problems

[27] Schneider, B. (1987). The people make the place. *Personnel Psychology*, 40, 437-454.
[28] Freeman, M. A., Staudenmaier, P. J., Zisser, M. R., & Andresen, L. A. (2019). The prevalence and co-occurrence of psychiatric conditions among entrepreneurs and their families. *Small Business Economics*, 53(2), 323-342.
[29] Andreasen, N. (20038, The relationship between creativity and mood disorders. *Dialogues in Clinical Neuroscience*, 10(2): p. 251-255.
[30] Salguero, J. M., Extremera, N., & Fernández-Berrocal, P. (2012). Emotional intelligence and depression: The moderator role of gender. *Personality and Individual Differences*, 53(1), 29-32.
[31] Karpinski, R. I., Kolb, A. M. K., Tetreault, N. A., & Borowski, T. B. (2018). High intelligence: A risk factor for psychological and physiological overexcitabilities. *Intelligence*, 66, 8-23.
[32] Nesse, R. M. (2000). Is depression an adaptation?. *Archives of general psychiatry*, 57(1), 14-20

that require long periods of time, attention, and realistic thinking.

ADHD: Dopamine receptor genes—responsible for novelty-seeking and other curious qualities of the entrepreneurial spirit—have long been associated with ADHD.[33] While America is quick to medicate symptoms of inattention, many entrepreneurs view their ADHD diagnosis as an invaluable advantage that offers opportunity recognition and innovative achievement,[34] risk taking,[35] action orientation,[36] and heightened entrepreneurial intentions.[37] And, despite popular belief, individuals with ADHD actually have the ability to *hyper-focus* on subjects they're particularly interested in.[38]

Addiction: The dopamine receptor genes implicated in addiction may also provide the entrepreneur with enhanced novelty-seeking, sensation-seeking, and risk-seeking tendencies.[39] Entrepreneurs often walk the fine line between passion and obsession, and while addiction is admittedly not an ideal state in which to find oneself, the entrepreneur with addictive tendencies may prove parti-

---

[33] Cornish, K. M., Manly, T., Savage, R., Swanson, J., Morisano, D. Association of the dopamine transporter (DAT1) 10/10-repeat genotype with ADHD symptoms and response inhibition in a general population sample. *Molecular psychiatry*. 2005; 10(7), 686.

[34] White, H.A., & Shah, P. (2006). Uninhibited imaginations: Creativity in adults with attention-deficit/hyperactivity disorder. *Personality and Individual Differences*, 40, 1121-1131.

[35] Mantyla, T., Still, J., Gullberg, S., & Del Missier, F. (2012). Decision making in adults with ADHD. *Journal of Attention Disorders*, 16, 164-173.

[36] Flach, F. (1997). Disorders of the pathways involved in the creative process. *Eminent creativity, everyday creativity, and health*, 179-189.

[37] Verheul, I., Block, J., Burmeister-Lamp, K., Thurik, R., Tiemeier, H., & Turturea, R. (2015). ADHD-like behavior and entrepreneurial intentions. *Small Business Economics*, 45, 85-101.

[38] Hupfeld, K. E., Abagis, T. R., & Shah, P. (2019). Living "in the zone": hyperfocus in adult ADHD. *ADHD Attention Deficit and Hyperactivity Disorders*, 11(2), 191-208.

[39] Lusher, J. M., Chandler, C., & Ball, D. (2001). Dopamine D4 receptor gene (DRD4) is associated with Novelty Seeking (NS) and substance abuse: the saga continues... *Molecular Psychiatry*, 6(5), 497-499.

cularly devoted and impassioned in the face of adversity and challenge.

Bipolar: While bipolar may be the most "feared" of the diagnoses, many a brilliant mind has been touched by manic-depressive tendencies.[17] During manic periods, the entrepreneur may experience increased activity and energy,[40] as well as heightened pride, ability to improvise, proactivity, and extraversion.[41] During depressive periods, they become more focused and practical, which may allow them to focus on a single problem or task, like writing a book or coding an app.[32]

2. Nature of Entrepreneurial Work

In addition to the genetically-bestowed neurodiversity of entrepreneurs, the impact of their work must also be considered. While entrepreneurship is a uniquely rewarding type of work, it can pose significant threats to many aspects of an entrepreneur's health and well-being. Individuals who encounter severe or prolonged stress may "activate" an underlying predisposition for mental or physical illness—a phenomenon called Diathesis-Stress or Vulnerability-Stress—that can catalyze the

Self-Actualization: Fulfilling Potential
Failure, crisis of meaning, identity crisis

Esteem: Accomplishment
Competition, imposter syndrome

Belonging: Relationships
Isolation, no time for relationships

Safety: Security
Instability, uncertainty, lack of resources

Physiological: Food, water, rest
Extreme workload, lack of self-care, irregular sleep

---

[40] Machado-Vieira, R., Luckenbaugh, D. A., Ballard, E. D., Henter, I. D., Tohen, M., Suppes, T., & Zarate, C. A. (2017). Increased activity or energy as a primary criterion for the diagnosis of bipolar mania in DSM-5: findings from the STEP-BD study. *American Journal of Psychiatry, 174*(1), 70–76.
[41] Johnson, S. L., Madole, J. W., & Freeman, M. A. (2018). Mania Risk and Entrepreneurship: Overlapping Personality Traits. *Academy of Management Perspectives, 32*(2), 207–227.

development of a disorder.[42] In other words, when the stresses of entrepreneurship interact with the genetic vulnerability of entrepreneurs, they may be more likely to manifest mental or physical illness. To categorize these stressors, I've mapped them according to Maslow's Hierarchy of Needs:

> **Physiological:** Entrepreneurs often report lack of sleep due to stress or workload, skipped or non-nutritious meals, excessive use of stimulants like caffeine, excessive use of sedatives like alcohol, and insufficient time to exercise. Entrepreneurship is also known for its devotion and effort—often referred to as "hustling"—and while extreme diligence and commitment can lead to success, these behaviors can rapidly deplete the entrepreneur's physiological resources. In fact, an entrepreneur's stress level is more affected by workload than other factors, like role ambiguity or underutilization of skills.[43]

> **Safety:** Entrepreneurs face both acute and chronic threats to their sense of safety. They are exposed to high levels of uncertainty and risk, and often face unstable financial, human, and emotional resources,[44] all of which can activate the body's sympathetic nervous system. Over time, this chronic fight-or-flight response can trigger inflammatory processes that promote mental and physical illness.

> **Love/Belonging:** Particularly in the early days of a venture, entrepreneurship can be a surprisingly isolating endeavor.[45]

[42] Hankin, B. L., & Abela, J. R. (Eds.). (2005). *Development of psychopathology: A vulnerability-stress perspective.* Sage.

[43] Harris, J. A., Saltstone, R., & Fraboni, M. (1999). An evaluation of the job stress questionnaire with a sample of entrepreneurs. *Journal of Business and Psychology, 13*(3), 447-455.

[44] Koudstaal, M., Sloof, R., & Van Praag, M. (2015). Risk, uncertainty, and entrepreneurship: Evidence from a lab-in-the-field experiment. *Management Science, 62*(10), 2897-2915.

[45] Sexton, D.L. (1985). The entrepreneur: A capable executive and more. *Journal of business venturing, 1*(1), 129-140.

Many entrepreneurs report feelings of loneliness, and often struggle to make time for friends, family, and romantic relationships. Even when they're surrounded by others, many report feeling quite "lonely at the top,"[46] and a lack of social ties has been shown to detrimentally affect entrepreneurial well-being. Indeed, the economic stresses of entrepreneurship are more likely to lead to depression in entrepreneurs with few social ties than in those with more social ties.[47]

Esteem: More so than perhaps any other career, entrepreneurial success or failure has a weighty impact on one's self-esteem.[48] Between the unceasing pressure to compete and constant reminders of unattainable success, entrepreneurs often experience imposter syndrome and other threats to their self-esteem.[52]

Self-Actualization: Many entrepreneurs use their work as a means to self-actualize.[48] While entrepreneurship can be a highly effective means to authentically create, express oneself, and leave an impact, it can also transform work challenges, like a failure or acquisition, into an existential threat. These disruptions to the process of self-actualization are often followed by a crisis of meaning, identity crisis, or other forms of spiritual-existential distress.

---

[46] Swersky, P., Gorman, A., & Reardon, J. (2007). We've Got the Power: Rise of Women Entrepreneurs. *New England Journal of Public Policy, 22*(1), 7.

[47] Pollack, Jeffrey M., et al. "The Moderating Role of Social Ties on Entrepreneurs Depressed Affect and Withdrawal Intentions in Response to Economic Stress." *Journal of Organizational Behavior,* vol. 33, no. 6, 2012, pp. 789–810.

[48] Carland Jr, J. W., Carland, J. A. C., & Carland III, J. W. T. (1995). Self-actualization: The zenith of entrepreneurship. *Journal of Small Business Strategy, 6*(1), 53-66.

3. Culture of the Entrepreneurial Ecosystem

Finally, the role of entrepreneurial culture must be examined. As a historically male-dominated profession, entrepreneurship has long-been perceived as a masculine behavior,[50] and one could easily argue that the entrepreneurial ecosystem is largely rooted in the values and beliefs of the masculine archetype (note that masculine and

Qualities of Masculine Archetype	Qualities of Feminine Archetype
Discerning	Intuitive
Protective	Accepting
Reasoning	Feeling
Discriminating	Unifying
Distinction	Relationship
Boundaries	Wholeness
Structure	Beauty
Product	Process
	Source[49]

feminine archetypes aren't related to a gender, but rather represent qualities that every individual embodies to a greater or lesser extent). Among entrepreneurs, masculine qualities like authoritarianism, independence, and being "cutthroat"[51] tend to be respected more than feminine qualities like nurturance, collaboration, and creativity,[49] and this reliance on the masculine archetype has likely bred the ecosystem's pervasive "hustle" culture. It's anecdotally popular for entrepreneurs to practice a distorted form of Stoicism in which they fail to acknowledge and express negative emotions, fearing that this lack of "resilience" will make them appear weak, and many adopt a puritanical work ethic that has self-flagellating effects on their body and mind. This culture of masculinity—often *toxic* masculinity—can exacerbate an entrepreneur's physical, mental, emotional, and spiritual distress by not only placing more stress on the individual, but by preventing them from seeking the help they truly need. This may be particularly true for female creators who often discount themselves as not "real"

---

[49] Baker, Carolyn. *Collapsing Consciously: Transformative Truths for Turbulent Times.* North Atlantic Books, 2013.

[50] Balachandra, L., Briggs, A. R., Eddleston, K., & Brush, C. (2013). Pitch like a man: Gender stereotypes and entrepreneur pitch success. *Frontiers of Entrepreneurship Research, 33*(8), 2.

[51] Guzie, T., & Guzie, N. M. (1984). Masculine and feminine archetypes: A complement to the psychological types. *Journal of Psychological Type, 7,* 3-11.

entrepreneurs because they cannot understand how to succeed amidst these hyper-masculine norms.[52]

"Male and female represent the two sides of the great radical dualism. But in fact they are perpetually passing into one another. Fluid hardens to solid, solid rushes to fluid. There is no wholly masculine man, no purely feminine woman."
— Margaret Fuller

A Personal & Social Imperative

"Only when we are brave enough to explore the darkness will we discover the infinite power of our light."
—Brené Brown

I'm occasionally asked why I've chosen to focus my work on entrepreneurs, a population that, on the surface, may seem relatively privileged. To that question, I have a few responses. As an entrepreneurial spirit myself, I have embodied all of these creators—in both light and quite shadowy forms—and have dedicated myself to a lifelong journey of self-study. I'm far from perfect, and the work of an entrepreneurial spirit is a *life's* work, but through my darkest moments I have learned how to move, bit by bit, toward wholeness. My background justifies my work in this field, having held jobs in psychology, neuroscience, startups, venture capital, and mindfulness, but in the words of one of my dearest teachers, *You can never take someone somewhere that you haven't been yourself.* In my mind, the most important credentials I possess come from my own journey in learning how to create with mental, emotional, physical, and spiritual well-being. There is no substitute for the path itself.

But beyond my deep love for and resonance with entrepreneurial spirits, there's another reason I'm so drawn to this work. Creators

---

[52] Ladge, J., Eddleston, K. A., & Sugiyama, K. (2019). Am I an entrepreneur? How imposter fears hinder women entrepreneurs' business growth. *Business Horizons.*

have an enormous impact on the development of humankind on a global scale, and the mental, emotional, physical, and spiritual well-being of entrepreneurs isn't just a concern for entrepreneurs—it's a concern for humanity. Entrepreneurship is at the heart of social and economic growth, and is responsible for everything from job creation to social trends to the adoption of new technologies by the collective.[53] Entrepreneurial spirits create the next version of reality for *all* of us, and if the source code isn't functioning properly, there's little hope for the end result. While every human is responsible for leaving their mark on this world, entrepreneurial spirits are often the ones who do so at scale and therefore have the potential to leave the largest impact—positive *or* negative. Recent news has been littered with examples of creators behaving "badly," and these failings, while personal, also have an impact on the broader social, cultural, and economic landscape. It's in the best interest of the collective to invest in the fountainhead of the creative process: the entrepreneur.

By investing in the well-being of creators, we invest in the future of humanity. If we want to create a happy and healthy future, we must ensure the designers of that future are happy and healthy too. The ability to influence global trends is not a responsibility to be taken lightly, and I believe that all entrepreneurs should be as eagerly armed with the tools to take care of themselves as they are their companies. By encouraging the development of self-awareness in entrepreneurs, they will inevitably create products that reflect this heightened awareness. Creators are patient zero of our modern day breakthroughs and epidemics—they are the parents from which all creations and their consequences spring forth. If key stakeholders, like investors, universities, policymakers, and the like, begin to see the individual creator as this most critical starting point, they will inevitably be compelled to shift their investment strategies: instead of investing in products once they are built, they might begin to see

---

[53] Van Praag, C. M., & Versloot, P. H. (2007). What is the value of entrepreneurship? A review of recent research. *Small business economics, 29*(4), 351-382.

value in investing at the source. Elevating the intentionality of products is a nice goal, but is a rather clumsy and inefficient effort when the ecosystem could be elevating the consciousness of creators themselves.

While the capacity for self-awareness and emotional intelligence may seem like a nicety rather than an entrepreneurial neccessity, this view is woefully misinformed. Emotional intellience in entrepreneurs is correlated with entrepreneurial skills like decision making, creativity, emotional resilience, motivation, leadership, and calculated risk-taking, and it's well past time to offer educational resources that not only attend to the hard-skills of entre-preneurship, but the crucial soft-skills as well.[54] Without cultivating the emotional landscape of the entrepreneur, they are left ill-prepared for the inevitable battles ahead. In the same way that a scalpel and the designation of doctor isn't handed to a young person who lacks proper training, a startup manual shouldn't be thrust into the hands of creators with the instruction to simply "build a business." While I value the improvisational and opportunistic nature of entrepreneurial work, the responsibility to influence the world at scale shouldn't be taken lightly—the consequences of a creator's consciousness or lack thereof affect the collective in innumerable, deeply meaningful ways. It's not enough to be intellectually prepared for new venture creation; entre-preneurs must also be emotionally prepared. There are far too many examples of creators lacking in emotional regulation tools who harm themselves, their bottom line, their investors, their customers, their employees, and others around them in the process of building a business—they really don't have to make such a mess of things.

> *"There is a strong shadow where this is much light."*
> — *Johann Wolfgang von Goethe*

---

[54] Ghosh, N. B., & Rajaram, G. (2015). Developing emotional intelligence for entrepreneurs: The role of entrepreneurship development programs. *South Asian Journal of Management, 22*(4), 85-100.

A Final Point

"Love all the ones who you are, and then you will know how to love the world."
— Elizabeth Gilbert

As I began interviewing entrepreneurs for this book, I quickly realized I didn't want to use the stories of "celebrity" entrepreneurs. There are no nods to household innovators, and this omission is very intentional: I wanted the stories used in this book to reflect the vulnerable experiences of everyday creators, some of whom became "unicorns" and others who never raised more than a few thousand dollars. To maintain the honesty and integrity of these journeys, all of the stories are of creators I've befriended, worked alongside, and dated, and all of their names and identifying information have been changed to respect their privacy. I've had the honor of witnessing the highs and lows of their journeys firsthand, and am able to share their stories without minced words or glossed-over truths. I'm deeply thankful for each and every entrepreneurial spirit who has inspired and continues to inspire me—the stories that they feel are most isolating and shameful are indeed the ones that are most universal.

Before we journey into Part II—the exploration of the creators within the entrepreneurial spirit—I have one more chapter to share. It's my own story. I don't share my story to make this book about me, for it surely would have been less problematic to leave this chapter out. The words that follow are hard for me to write—they are messy, vulnerable, and at times, rather ugly—but it's important that you know that I too am on this journey with you. I offer my story to underscore how crucial the practices of self-understanding, self-acceptance, and self-care are for creators. I offer it as a reminder that I am both a teacher and a student. I offer it as a demonstration that I can stand—safely and with strength—in my own untidy truth. I offer it as a promise that I have fallen ... hard ... and have risen back up with nothing but deep love and embodied respect for you as a spectacularly complex entrepreneurial spirit.

"What makes night within us may leave stars."
— Victor Hugo

Chapter 3:
Creator, Interrupted

"What is most personal is most universal."
— Carl Rogers

When I was a little girl, I was a most wild and uninhibited creator. This isn't to say I was rambunctious or particularly naughty, but I truly delighted in the act of creation. I grew up in farm country and was lucky enough to have a mother who didn't overstuff my schedule with to-do's and forced fun, which freed up bountiful time to think, explore, play, and create. I donned overalls without undergarments, was covered in dirt more often than not, almost never wore shoes, and loved nothing more than creating something from nothing. Gangly and shaped rather like a beanpole, my hair was always a golden, tangled mess, and my saucer-sized blue eyes viewed every object or situation as something that could be easily transformed into a creative plaything. My father's empty cardboard boxes became tables for restaurants, construction paper became tickets to backyard fairs and bug museums, and anything that remotely resembled a school supply was immediately refurbished for use in my pretend schoolhouse. Like a little witch with a wand, I cast spells upon everything so that hamsters became business partners and dolls became surgical patients, and I spent hour upon countless hour absorbed in a colorful world of my own making.

My childhood self—perhaps more so than any later version of myself—was a pure and healthy conduit for creation, and I gladly let myself be used as a vessel to bring new *stuff* into the world. With the ease of changing into a costume—of which I had many—I transformed myself into a myriad of personas boasting their own creative gifts. I played teacher, spending hours with my imaginary students who all had their own personalities, full of C+ quirks and punishable mischievousness. I played doctor, relishing the idea of healing my patients who almost always had scarlet fever, which I believed to be the worst condition one could have. I played storekeeper, creating markets and restaurants in which I charged my customer—my bright-eyed little sister—exorbitant rates for plastic fruits and vegetables, payable by plastic coins and bright green paper money. I relished time alone in my playroom—my sanctuary—where I effortlessly molded and shaped my world into any creative reality that pleased me. Uninhibited and unconcerned by the *shoulds* of the world, I was a most productive creator.

A strong-willed yet deeply sensitive child, my inspiration often came to me in the form of intangible ideas, sensations, and emotions, and I had a funny way of fitting in everywhere and nowhere. Empathic, intuitive, introverted, and a deep feeler, I sensed the energy in everyone and everything, dreamed vividly, and was acutely aware—often to my own detriment—of the world around me. I loved animals deeply, often preferring their company to the company of rowdy children, and even though other children readily accepted me, I spent the majority of my childhood by myself, blissfully content with my time for reflection and play. Spring and summer were endless days of make-believe and hiding under the willow tree in the backyard listening to the cicadas, and fall and winter were cozy pauses made for snuggling with books and eating treat after treat that my lanky body seemed to metabolize into thin air. I questioned the way things were and the way people behaved, and much to my parents' annoyance, I often embodied a little philosopher and psychologist, even going so far as to play priestess in my bedroom. While I had my own endearing ticks and idiosyncrasies as a child, manifesting obsessive little routines like locking doors and washing hands, or being so intense and contemplative that I was jokingly called "Oscar the Grouch," I was content in my reflective way of living and creating, and couldn't imagine myself any other way.

Until one day—the day that comes sooner or later for every child—the voices of the creators within grew quiet. One morning, as I was teaching my classroom of students—a particularly troublesome group—I looked out at my playroom of makeshift tables and white sheets of printer paper with grades scribbled on them, and it dawned on me for the first time I was talking to an empty room. I felt a pang of self-conscious silliness as I turned to the chalkboard to restart my lecture, only to be reminded of the empty room that silently laughed behind my back. I feared nothing more than looking immature, so I left my playroom, pronouncing that I wanted to be a grown-up, *not* a child. Little did I know I was leaving play behind both literally and metaphorically, and was symbolically stepping away from my creative spirit. I didn't sense it at the time, but it would be a long, *long* journey back home.

Over the following years, I came to be praised not for my creativity, but for my intellect. I was celebrated as a natural student, and, in a rather slow and accidental way, I began to replace my love of creation with a love of learning, assuming they were surely different things. I retired my kid games for debate teams, spelling bees, and student council, and quickly came to enjoy the validation that bright stickers on homework assignments and red safety-patrol vests offered. Before I knew it, I began to operate not from my heart, but from my precocious little head. Things carried on in this way for a while without much fuss or concern, and my childhood bedroom that was once decorated with drawings and toys slowly transformed into a teenager's room with plaques and awards. Even though I felt there was something a little *off*, something *missing,* in this new way of life, I ignored these intuitive squirmings, and proudly declared a career that sounded most impressive: I wanted to be a doctor. So, I replaced my art supplies with microscopes and fiction books with anatomy texts, and stubbornly decided it was time to grow up. There was no room for play anymore.

I settled on neuroscience as my lofty study of choice and dove headfirst into my college years studying neurotransmitters and synapses. A fiercely diligent worker bee, I puffed my chest with pride when I was accepted as an undergraduate researcher in one of the most prestigious neuroscience laboratories at the National Institutes of Health. I was tasked with scanning brains and running studies, and I felt so pleased with myself as I flashed my badge at the security post each morning—*I'm finally a grown-up*, I thought. But even though I relished the validation I received when I told people I was a neuroscience researcher—savoring the lofty intelligence and maturity it implied—I was far from captivated with my work. There was no space for creativity, spontaneity, or improvisation—at least, not in the lab I worked in—and the routinized nature of the work soon began to feel like nothing short of sensory deprivation. Before long, lost in a sea of my own boredom and fidgety discontent, I started to deprive something other than my senses.

It was never my intention to lose weight. As an awkwardly thin child and teenager who wore the slimmest jeans in every store, I didn't begin to control my eating to further slenderize my figure. Instead, as disordered eating often does, it started as an innocent pledge to eat healthy. While I was working at NIH, pushing full-steam ahead toward a career that my inner-child knew I didn't want, I began to replace my daily bacon, egg, and cheese bagel from the campus deli with fresher, "cleaner" options. *I'm an adult who is learning to take care of herself*, I said. Before long, my healthy preferences waded into pescatarianism. And then vegetarianism. And then veganism. And then, before I knew it, I found myself eating little more than raw fruits and veggies, and any low-calorie treat I could get my hands on. At the time, I really didn't see what was happening—I didn't let myself see it. After a few months of these cruel games of control, my fragile, emaciated body barely had the life force to transport itself from one end of NIH's sprawling campus to the other. Nonetheless, I insisted that my weakness and fatigue were surely due to some undiagnosed medical condition, and refused to accept that *I* had created this awful version of reality. Though all of my bodies—physical, mental, emotional, and spiritual—were dramatically dissociated from each other, it was only through the horrified look in my parents' eyes that I realized that something was really, *really* wrong.

And so I "recovered" through a self-imposed diet of peanut butter, and like a cartoon character being blown up with air, my body came alive again. In true form, I graduated college with a perfect GPA and nothing but smiles, having never taken time away to actually recover. Upon graduation, I once again accepted a role in a laboratory at the NIH, this time as a full-time Research Fellow. Stepping back into the clinical floor for a second go-round, I could see the relieved look on the clinicians' faces when they saw my pants were no longer hanging off of my protruding hipbones and my big blue-green eyes, flecked with yellow, no longer sunk into my hollow face. But what they didn't know was that I had only addressed the very surface of what needed healing—I had *played* patient more than I had actually *been* a patient. While I made my body look "normal" again, I hadn't touched the root source of my troubles. In hindsight, it's clear how the distress I was experiencing was a result of me hiding in my shadows—over-working, over-performing, over-analyzing as a way to escape my creative light—but it was going to take a few more dark nights for me to learn that lesson.

After a year or so in the lab, I once again found myself fighting against my alarm clock and begrudgingly dragging myself into the office. I ignored my squirming thoughts and emotions once again, and, like clockwork, my body creatively stepped in to get my attention. One day, as I was given a new assignment that would require me to stay in the laboratory for at least another year, I felt a wave of *death* come over me. I couldn't catch my breath, didn't know where my body started and stopped, and was certain my heart was about to explode. Fortunately, I was not dying but was instead having a panic attack, right there in the middle of the lab. Yet, despite this laughably unsubtle signal from my body, I stubbornly dug my heels in deeper and deeper into this path of sameness and control. It truly didn't occur to me at the time that my body was acting out—nay, *pleading*—for a kind of nourishment I wasn't offering it. My spirit was begging for expression and authenticity, bucking at a path so devoid of creativity and self-directedness. As the months passed, I realized that even though I had worked so hard to get to this point, I had to turn around and start again. Despite my own protests—of which there were many—I knew it was time for me to return to that bright little spirit within.

I was dating Jason while working at the NIH, and he was the first to see not only my apathy toward my work but my suffocated entrepreneurial spirit that wanted an outlet for expression. In a thoughtful and generous way, he nudged me to explore entrepreneurship, suggesting that it would be a fulfilling alignment of my personality, interests, and strengths, and perhaps out of both an inner knowing and a desire to impress my first real-world beau, I decided that he was right. In one of the most impulsive decisions I'd ever made—the first of what would turn out to be many—I quit my job at the NIH without having another role lined up, and began the process of searching for a position at a startup. This turned out to not be an easy feat in D.C.'s then-infant ecosystem, and much to my dismay, I struggled to find a job. I tripped over myself as I met with prospective employers and unsuccessfully explained that I had no business experience whatsoever, but instead had an impressive albeit irrelevant pedigree in academia. Although I found myself distressed about my newfound unemployment, a rather incredible thing began to happen—my creativity started to blossom once again. I created a blog, adorned myself in colorful clothing, and even dipped my toe into a brand-new world of yoga and mindfulness. And before long, my opportunity to claim my power as a creator arose from out of the blue.

One night while out with a friend, we found ourselves at a launch party for a new, social-professional networking startup, and quite by accident, I found myself in a conversation with the founder. He immediately took a liking to me, and offered me a job a few days later to launch the D.C. chapter, the largest community outside the founding city. While I had no idea what I was doing, I eagerly said yes, and in no small way, it was one of the most expanding experiences of my life. In a role that had the freedom of a founder and the security of employment, I learned how to wear every different hat, play every different role, and all of the creators within me began to speak. I learned to be a marketer, content creator, event planner, community leader, business development professional, operations coordinator, and a mess of other roles that filled me with unbridled energy and inspiration. I started to write in a deeply authentic way, and before long, I had somehow become a minor celebrity in D.C.'s entrepreneurial ecosystem. And no one was more surprised by this than I.

As a lifelong introvert who was woefully unaccustomed to the glitzy social world, I frequently locked myself in bathroom stalls to take a breather from the intense stimulation of events and parties. At first, I felt rather like an alien when people suddenly wanted to know who I was, and this filled me with both pride and admittedly overwhelm. But what started out as true imposter syndrome began to morph into brazen empowerment, and, seemingly overnight, this oft-awkward, empathic girl found herself as a mercurial, self-interested woman. My friends became a circle of socialites who looked nice in photos, my weekends were characterized by velvet ropes and bottle service, and my workdays weren't complete without articles that celebrated my young success story. I began to relish and expect the attention, and once again, my creative endeavors began to slip and slide down my list of priorities. Before long, I was invited to join a D.C.-based venture firm in a role that seemed lofty for both my age and my gender, and at the time, there was nothing more validating than adding the title "VC" to my resume. Without giving it too much thought, I was delighted to accept.

More quickly than I ever could have imagined, I found myself living in a man's world. I was a young doe in a forest full of bucks, and I was *really* proud of that fact. Venture capital is a strange, sweaty land for a 24-year-old to find herself, and I found that everything oozed and dripped with masculinity. It was as if the scent of virile power was pumped through the pipes, and the whole game thrived off the energy of stoicism, action, and aggression. While the colleagues in my venture firm were surprisingly kind and supportive, I came to believe that any remaining aspects of my creative, feminine nature had to be pressed out like wrinkles if I was to fit in, and, as I'm wont to do, I went to extremes. My closet full of delicate, flowy clothing was tossed away in favor of black tops and smart flats, and I began to consume startup and venture content over anything remotely whimsical. Within a few months of working in venture capital, I aligned myself decidedly with the masculine, and I was really pleased with my newfound warrior energy.

I relished my status as a member of the boys club, and was willing to do anything necessary to fit in and maintain good standing, so I drank the brown booze, smoked the cigars, and barreled my way through meetings. No one ever questioned me when I walked into rooms with powerful influencers who were 20, 30, or 40 years my senior. *Finally*, I thought with glee, *they had lost track of my scent*. I giggled at the image of me smearing myself with musk, knocking on the door with skinned knees and a just-harsh-enough tongue to earn entry into the clubhouse. I looked the other way as men made inappropriate passes at me, and considered their offers of money and guidance so I could start my own company, even though I found this generosity to be slimily laden with contingencies. I felt that my tolerance of their distorted power and weak masculinity was not just a nicety, but a necessity, and I worried that I wouldn't be accepted, much less respected, if I challenged the rules that were clearly laid out before me. So, I leveraged my adaptive, open-minded, and apparently charismatic nature to create a new persona that was brilliantly suited for this ecosystem, ignoring the fact that this persona was a rather dark shadow of the bright little spirit who was still trying to find her way to the light.

As I waded further into this masquerade, I quickly began to transform into a rather unhappy warrior. I "hustled" and "crushed it" and assumed that anyone who didn't work as hard as I did was a lost cause. My instinct to succeed warped into hyper-competitiveness, and I began to demand raises and promotions that I admittedly hadn't earned. Testing the boundaries of my newfound masculine energy, I often found myself in trouble for my feistily-worded emails and tense kerfuffles with colleagues, and it felt as though no level of status or achievement would satisfy me. My knee jerked with resentment every time I saw an "Under 30" list, choosing to look the other way when others were praised for their well-earned success, and I increasingly kept myself far, *far* away from other women—especially accomplished women. I deemed it a survival tactic to suppress my feelings, so I learned to keep a sturdy upper lip and maintain a façade of stoic resilience, despite my body's pleas to process the mini traumas I was inflicting upon it. Although it was a combustive game, I suppose I was successful because no one ever presumed I was anything but *fine*. In the evening, I'd go home and try to cry in front of a mirror, but like a bad actress, I just sat there waiting for tears to fall that never came.

Soon, these extreme tendencies that I deemed to be a requirement of my day job began to permeate my whole life. Consciously or unconsciously, I aligned my body, mind, and demeanor fully with who I *thought* I needed to be to succeed as a modern-day creator: tough, impressive, and charming despite the truth. Quite maddeningly, every misstep and moment of inauthenticity was celebrated, and I was never more praised or followed than in my darkest moments. I was slapped with congratulatory labels that encouraged my imbalances, like "boss woman" or "lady hustler," and grew hopelessly confused about who I was and what I wanted. But eventually, the dissonance between who I am pretending to be and who I was meant to be grew too cacophonous, and every single one of my strengths as a creator started to backfire and self-combust: my openness transformed into indecision, intuition into overwhelm, achievement motivation into exhaustion, healthy ego into a weak ego, passion into obsession, conscientiousness into control, charisma into inauthenticity, disagreeability into aggression, optimism into delusion, and desire to self-actualize into a crisis of meaning. Somehow, all of my most celebrated qualities as a creator—my feistiness, work ethic, and ability to shapeshift—were the very causes of my crisis. I was a creator, interrupted.

By this time, my body had had enough. And now, it knew it needed to become *extra* creative. Quite symbolically—for no apparent reason on some not so special day—my long, flowing hair began to fall out. Strand by strand, my golden locks began to betray their rightful home on my proud little head, and instead fell quite noticeably on the shoulders of my black shirts. Big yellow dust bunnies of hair collected in the corners of my apartment, and I stuffed down my anger and confusion as I brushed strands off my keyboard while typing emails to venture partners. I would later learn that hair is not only symbolic of femininity, but also of instinct, freedom, power, strength, creativity, and spirituality, and medieval witches—or "wise woman" and "feminine creators"—had their hair shorn as way to strip them of their power. Though it didn't take a witch doctor to pick up on this clever symbolism—a golden canary in the coalmine—I nevertheless ignored this strange phenomenon for months until I began suffering from a mess of other unglamorous physical, emotional, mental, and spiritual symptoms. Of all of the ugly evidence, perhaps most telling was that I stopped dreaming at night, my intuitive hunches grew forebodingly silent, and the color had literally and symbolically melted out of my life.

As the months passed, it became increasingly clear that this issue wasn't going to resolve itself, and I began a melancholic spiral downward. I fell into a deep inner crisis—complete with a collection of obsessive, depressive, ruminatory, and manic tendencies—and battled the darkest and cruelest night of the soul. I couldn't understand what was happening, how to fix it, or where to go for help. *I only did what they wanted me to do*, I thought. I felt distrustful of everyone and everything, and grew to resent my body, mind, and spirit that so violently betrayed me. I felt all alone, overwhelmed, and far from home without any breadcrumbs to find my way back. I went to doctor after doctor, healer after healer, and no one could tell me why I was suffering or how I could find solace, and I grasped desperately at golden threads, wanting to find some tangible diagnosis or explanation for my symptoms. But alas, no justification or validation came, and I was left to put together the pieces on my own. I felt as if I had wandered a million miles away from that sweet creator who had once joyfully and easily manifested her reality, and more than anything else in the world, I just wanted her tiny bright spirit back.

As a rather stubborn being, it was as if my body knew that the only way I would listen was to induce something so scarring, so humiliating, so isolating. Burnout doesn't begin to describe the emotional, mental, physical, and spiritual anguish I suffered at my own hand, and as the months passed, it became undeniably clear that the only way out was through—the only person who could save me was myself. Finally, after countless sleepless nights and curled-up protests on my bathroom floor, I decided to take this call to action seriously. The comically extreme nature of my lessons was necessary for me to learn, and I spent the following years immersed in bottomless healing work that was largely self-driven and entirely focused on understanding my own complexities. From psychology to various healing modalities to ancient wisdom traditions, I chose to devote myself to self-study so that I could return to the status that is my birthright—to be a pure and healthy conduit for creation.

At first, it was a messy and clumsy process, like a little animal learning to walk for the first time, but rather quickly, I retrained my muscles and began to stand upright in my creative power once again. As I began to honor the creators within myself and step back into the fullness of my creative, empathic, and intuitive gifts, I began to heal on every level quite naturally. This was the medicine that my spirit forced me to swallow, and now on the other side, I feel it's my responsibility to share these lessons with others. For anyone who has ever looked at me or who will read this book and think, *She has it all together*, the truth is that the only knowledge I have is born from my struggles and my embodiment as my *own* healer. There is no end to the process of becoming whole, and I—just like you—will continue to experience highs and lows, triumphs and lessons, bright days and dark nights. But I've come to learn that true success as an entrepreneurial spirit comes when we integrate all of the creators within us, and learn to honor our potentialities that demand expression. In the words of William James, "When an organism fails to fulfill its potentialities, it becomes sick," and it's my deepest hope that you learn to identify and express your potentialities before any mental, emotional, physical, or spiritual distress can take hold.

While I have embraced many healing modalities that ring true for me—meditation, dream work, painting, nature, yoga, poetry, reiki, music, massage, and more—these are but a few of the myriad tools that can be used in the process of self-study. There is no single path. Once I began to clearly see my light and dark, and acknowledge that my greatest challenges arise from my greatest strengths, I could see that I was not only already whole, but that I was bursting at the seams with gorgeous, quirky nuance! What child-like joy I felt when I realized the things I loved and hated about myself, the things I was celebrated and condemned for, were actually one in the same. The good and the bad—there was no difference—all of it was me. It was *always* me and I needed to use *all* of myself to create. I realized that I needed to step into my fullness—murkiness and all—if I was going to create a life that was healing for me and others around me. And so, I humbly offer you this book to make your journey a bit less painful and bit more joyous, and while we all have to experience challenges to find our own way, I hope that your path has much softer, squishier landings. I don't share anything in this book that I don't know intimately myself, and if just one spirit feels comforted by these stories, then I've succeeded in integrating my light and dark through the process of creation. And that, I've learned after all these years, is the whole point.

(P.S. My magical golden locks grew back into
their full abundance.)

"My speech is neither light nor dark, it is the speech of someone who
is growing."
— C.G. Jung

PART II:
The Creators

"I am one powerful self made up of so many selves
that sometimes I throw myself a get-acquainted party."
—Eric Maisel

The Creator Archetypes

The Curious Creator		
Dimension: Openness to experience	Light Qualities	Dark Qualities
• Deep and creative thinking • Novelty-seeking & sensation-seeking • Intellectual curiosity • Drawn to complex people and stimuli • Broad range of interests • Attention to inner feelings • Openness to absorption, hypnosability & self-transcendence • Interest in intense social, intellectual, physical & artistic stimuli • Tendency to be socially, politically & sexually liberal	Spontaneous; adventurous; free-thinking; thrill & novelty seeking; creative; unconventional; playful; perceptive; expressive; adaptive; artistic; ideational	Unpredictable; distracted; impulsive; fantastical; peculiar; unstable; flaky; restless; malleable; indulgent; unusual; unrelatable
Motivation: To explore and express **Mantra:** Leave no stone unturned **Tension:** Exploration vs. distraction	**To Integrate** Commitment	

The Sensitive Creator

Dimension: Intuition	**Light Qualities**	**Dark Qualities**
• Emotional intelligence • Self-awareness • Ability to sense feelings of others • Observationality & perceptivity • Sensitivity to environment & substances • Introversion with deep relationships • Creativity & rich inner world • Ability to see patterns and trends	Instinctive; sensitive; aware; empathic; inspired; attentive; observant; independent; emotional; insightful	Ungrounded; overstimulated; overwhelmed; depleted; irrational; disconnected; isolated; reactive; drained
Motivation: To connect the dots **Mantra:** Follow your gut **Tension:** Inspiration vs. overstimulation	**To Integrate** Grounding	

The Ambitious Creator

Dimension: Achievement motivation	**Light Qualities**	**Dark Qualities**
• Tendency to master subjects • Desire to demonstrate abilities • Strong work ethic • Striving for improvement • Interest in developing competency • Determination to be successful	Driven; performative; motivated; competitive; aspiring; forceful; go-getting; diligent; expectant	Exhausted; comparative; disappointed; self-critical; unrealistic; strained; overzealous; impatient
Motivation: To work hard and win fast **Mantra:** Hustle harder **Tension:** Acceleration vs. exhaustion	**To Integrate** Patience	

The Disruptive Creator

Dimension: Disagreeability	Light Qualities	Dark Qualities
• Willingness to risk social disapproval • Tendency to be confrontational • Critical-mindedness • Bluntness to the point of harshness • Unwillingness to cooperate and follow rules • Desire to challenge the status quo	Assertive; critical; blunt; innovative; stubborn; change-oriented; willful; feisty; headstrong; skeptical; free-thinking	Antagonistic; judgmental; unkind; defiant; loner; discontent; distant; combative; uncooperative; suspicious
Motivation: To challenge assumptions **Mantra:** Disrupt the status quo **Tension:** Innovation vs. destruction	**To Integrate** Gratitude	

The Empowered Creator

Dimension: Ego	Light Qualities	Dark Qualities
• Confidence in one's abilities • Feelings of self-worth and respect • Positive beliefs and emotions about oneself • High resilience and adaptability • Sense of authentic personal power • Motivation to achieve and to win • Ability to be responsible and accountable	Self-assured, confident; impactful; responsible; resilient; effective; accountable; leader; commanding; proud	Selfish; arrogant; vain; grandiose; domineering; prideful; delusional; insecure; defensive; validation-seeking; condescending
Motivation: To claim power **Mantra:** I am worthy **Tension:** Assurance vs. arrogance	**To Integrate** Values	

The Fiery Creator

Dimension: Passion	Light Qualities	Dark Qualities
• Increased motivation and drive • Positive emotions like pride and love • Willingness to take initiative • Enhanced mental activity and creativity • Feelings of meaning and importance • Willingness to explore risky opportunities • Preference for passion over reason	Devoted; impassioned; intense; absorbed; embodied; engrossed; committed; steadfast	Obsessed; consumed; dysregulated; self-sacrificing; crazed; unconditional; blinded; feverish; delirious
Motivation: To be energized **Mantra:** Live your passion **Tension:** Devotion vs. obsession	**To Integrate** Boundaries	

The Orderly Creator

Dimension: Conscientiousness	Light Qualities	Dark Qualities
• Strong self-discipline • Orderly processes • Reliability for important tasks • Industrious work ethic • Thorough deliverables • Attentiveness to detail • Desire to control outcomes	Attentive; organized; cautious; impeccable; deliberate; watchful; regimented; discriminating	Controlling; perfectionistic; anxious; hypervigilant; militant; compulsive; neurotic; fussy; untrusting
Motivation: To create order **Mantra:** Control your destiny **Tension:** Organization vs. perfectionism	**To Integrate** Trust	

The Charming Creator

Dimension: Charisma	Light Qualities	Dark Qualities
• Ability to attract, charm, influence, and evoke liking • Promotion of self and company as highly competent • Comradery with others • Use of smiling, flattery, and favors • Ability to sway others' beliefs • Tendency to project images of integrity	Convincing; persuasive; influential; accommodating; poised; magnetic; compelling; impressive; sociable	Manipulative; fake; insincere; disingenuous; conforming; suppressed; inauthentic; sneaky; deceitful; shrewd
Motivation: To woo and impress Mantra: Fake it till you make it Tension: Seduction vs. deception	To Integrate Authenticity	

The Courageous Creator

Dimension: Optimism	Light Qualities	Dark Qualities
• Hopefulness and emotional fortitude • Persistent action orientation • Positive explanatory style • Belief in positive or favorable outcomes • Enhanced creative & innovative thinking • Higher risk tolerance or risk preference	Brazen; decisive; daring; hopeful; resilient; positive; cheery; assured; spirited; upbeat; opportunistic; gritty; brave	Reckless; delusional; impulsive; blind; hasty; ignorant; foolhardy; uninhibited; rash; uninformed; immature
Motivation: To look on the bright side Mantra: Yes! Tension: Resilience vs. ignorance	To Integrate Intentionality	

The Existential Creator

Dimension: Self-Actualization	Light Qualities	Dark Qualities
• Expansion of personal boundaries • Realization of creative, intellectual & social potential • Experience of emotions like gratitude and awe • Belief in spiritual or greater sense of connectedness • Self-expression that is authentic and vulnerable • Feelings of meaning, fulfillment and wholeness • Tendency to be lost and absorbed by experience	Wise; serious; contemplative; soulful; fulfilled; intentional; reflective; grateful; mystical; philosophical; purposeful; impactful	Disillusioned; depressive; bitter; ruminative; hopeless; broody; heavy; unfulfilled; melancholy; pensive; dejected; discouraged; lost; haunted
Motivation: To find meaning **Mantra:** Live your purpose **Tension:** Realization vs. disillusion	**To Integrate** Joy	

Chapter 4:
The Curious Creator

The Curious Creator		
Dimension: Openness to experience	Light Qualities	Dark Qualities
• Deep and creative thinking • Novelty-seeking & sensation-seeking • Intellectual curiosity • Drawn to complex people and stimuli • Broad range of interests • Attention to inner feelings • Openness to absorption, hypnosability & self-transcendence • Interest in intense social, intellectual, physical & artistic stimuli • Tendency to be socially, politically & sexually liberal	Spontaneous; adventurous; free-thinking; thrill & novelty seeking; creative; unconventional; playful; perceptive; expressive; adaptive; artistic; ideational	Unpredictable; distracted; impulsive; fantastical; peculiar; unstable; flaky; restless; malleable; indulgent; unusual; unrelatable
Motivation: To explore and express **Mantra:** Leave no stone unturned **Tension:** Exploration vs. distraction	**To Integrate** Commitment	

An Indulgent Squirrel

Sam always had a way of keeping our friendship ... interesting.

Each day was met with a new proclamation: *I've decided to eat cricket powder and blueberries for a week. I want to scale volcanoes in Indonesia. I plan to sell my apartment and move to an ashram.* Sam's mind and body were always on the move, and he had a squirrelish energy that was at once playful and unnerving. With a frame that was 10 pounds lighter than it should have been from the caloric requirements of his constant fidgeting, he had a habit of chasing whatever person or idea was most interesting to him in that moment: his apartment was littered with half-opened packages that he impulse purchased in a fit of excitement and half-read books that he couldn't focus himself long enough to finish. Like a child who grew bored of a toy after an hour, Sam needed an enormous amount of newness and stimulation to be placated, and was appreciated not for his stability, but for his desire to turn life into one grand adventure. He was beloved for his fitful if not erratic qualities, and with windswept hair and big, wild eyes, he saw the blazing potential in every nook and cranny of reality.

I didn't really have a choice to become friends with Sam—he chose me. One afternoon during yoga, I grew acutely aware of the sensation of being watched, and, feeling a buzzing energy behind me, I turned around to see his slender frame and playful smirk aimed in my direction. Like a sprightly animal in search of a playmate, it seemed Sam wanted immediate companionship, and it was clear that when he set his sparkling blue eyes on someone or something, he wouldn't settle until he got it. After class, I saw his lithe self trailing me down the sidewalk on my way home, and within a matter of moments, he had solidified our status as friends. When I first discovered that Sam was the founder of a well-known startup, I was rather surprised that someone so open and unrestrained could run a company. However, my surprise quickly turned to understanding as I began to witness the extraordinary benefits of his wicked intelligence, unbiased receptivity, and free-thinking approach to life and work. It was as if his mind was a vacuum that sucked up new, exciting information, and, for better or worse, Sam was never not starving for more.

I'll never forget the first time I drove in a car with Sam: if he lived anything like the way he drove, I was in for a wild friendship. Sam took massive, indulgent bites out of his existence, and possessed a contagious *joie de vivre* that thrived on nonstop stimulation. Fun, playful, and always scampering around for his next thrill, Sam never wanted to do *normal* things, so to satisfy his own appetite for newness, we went on wild outings and once-in-a-lifetime adventures. With a terrible fear of missing out, he needed to be in the center of the action, and planned his own memorable, outlandish gatherings so as to never miss a moment of excitement. The launch party for his company was a rambunctious gathering that literally cost him the last dime in the bank, and when it came time to host his birthday, he planned an extravagant dinner complete with games that had adults chasing each other around a multimillion-dollar loft. Every one of Sam's gatherings was boisterous, provocative, and usually ended with someone crying in pain or joy, but when it was all over, things always worked out for him.

Sam's openness took him on magical experiences of his external *and* internal world, and he found deep dives into the stuff of his consciousness to be as exciting as any concert or vacation. He seemed to have no biases when it came to new perspectives, and whether it was a spiritual journey, a new business philosophy, or a counterculture political view, Sam held space to be everything and nothing at once. In the same way that he expected his experiences to thrill him with buzzy, novel sensations, he also expected his company to keep him on the edge of his seat, and it was as if he collected only the most intriguing souls along his journey. From rocket scientists to philosophers to famous thought leaders, his friends were a disparate stew of utterly fascinating and similarly open-minded individuals who could scratch his itch for tantalizing conversation and no holds barred living. Sam only had the patience for the most stimulating ideas and bleeding-edge humans, and like an indulgent squirrel, he wanted to shove *all* of life's acorns into his bursting cheeks.

While Sam's openness made him a fascinating dinner companion, it also offered him a special kind of curiosity and creativity that served his blossoming company well. Because newness didn't scare him, he was willing to make big, splashy changes that would have paralyzed others, and with a breathless eagerness to explore new ideas, he was constantly drawn to new people and opportunities that propelled his company forward. He made instinctive, emotionally-driven decisions that paid off more often than not, and created an experience for users with all the cheekiness and nuance that he wanted for himself. He could multitask like a madman and hold a million dissonant perspectives in his mind at once, and while you could never catch him on one train of thought, you could always rely on Sam to be a wellspring of new directions, fresh perspectives, and revised strategies. Indeed, when it came to his company, moss never grew under Sam's desk.

But over time, it became clear that Sam's openness was just as much of a liability as an asset. His colleagues complained of whiplash as he constantly changed direction, and Sam had a tendency of latching onto an idea of the moment—particularly if it was inspired by a mentor, friend, or investor he respected—even if it meant abandoning his previously cherished idea. While Sam thrived on newness, it perhaps didn't always occur to him that others preferred—nay, *required*—stability, and this resulted in tiffs big and small. Once something or someone grew boring, he became deathly claustrophobic and clawed his way out of the confines of dull ideas, roles, and strategies as if his sanity depended on it. It seemed that Sam's curiosity and novelty-seeking nature led to an optimization mentality—a constant attempt to find more interesting, exciting, and impressive opportunities—and this didn't bode well for his company *or* our friendship. It was almost as if life at its baseline state wasn't enough, and he found himself disappointed more often than not, bajiggity at the thought that there was always a more intriguing person, fabulous party, or interesting idea to attend to. Sam had a habit of scampering away when things got comfortable and darting back when the moment was properly sensational, and this created its fair share of bruised feelings and dinged egos.

For a while, I was hurt by the idea that I wasn't sensational enough for Sam, and though I could appreciate how his inner fidgeting was also his gift, I silently hoped that he would eventually find a bit more peace in the sweetness of stability and sameness. And over time, that's precisely what happened—a combination of time, experience, and meaningful life milestones began to tame Sam's openness, and he now has a quieter, more contained buzz about him. He has retreated to a life largely behind the scenes with his beloved wife, the one thing he couldn't let slip away, and while he still indulges in a life of newness and creativity, with the occasional impulse purchase and wild party, he has found the hinge point to balance his need for speed with stability. Wielding his curiosity with care if not impeccability, Sam is now mindful to collect his acorns while maintaining a safe and secure burrow for those around him. And, after all these years, he's managed to stay true to one of his most important commitments: his vision, his dream, and his sensational creation.

The Light

Perhaps more so than any other dimension in this book, openness to experience is met by an earnest, eager nod of knowing resonance from the entrepreneurial spirit. This open-hearted, often fidgety tendency is something the Curious Creator embodies in spades, leaving romantic partners and family members exasperated by their impassioned fits of excitement and compulsion to try everything once. The Curious Creator is familiar with the frustrated glances as they squirm their way through meetings, dive in and out of hobbies, toy with every possible perspective, and creatively concoct a version of reality that pleases them. Though they often frustrate others with their tendency to latch onto an idea, person, or interest of the moment, it seems the Curious Creator requires a more potent and diversified kind of fuel to run satisfactorily. While this openness can at times be an annoyance—breeding a persona that can appear flaky and eccentric at best—it's also the very source of their original, nonconforming, and complex minds.[55] As maddening as it may be at a social gathering or family dinner, the Curious Creator's openness to experience is really a restless blessing in disguise: it's the biological basis that explains their desire to put the whole world in their mouth.

Openness to experience is defined as the tendency to be imaginative, curious, spontaneous, expressive, novelty-seeking, and indeed, often distractible.[56] Openness reflects a receptivity to new experiences—from novel emotions to peculiar ideas to unfamiliar environments to unconventional values[61]—and the Curious Creator possesses an open mind that invites more information and stimuli into their system, allowing them to see the world more vividly and feel emotions—both positive and negative—more potently.[57] Indeed, the Curious Creator may require higher-than-normal levels of stimulation to find a satisfactory level of arousal, and need more stimulating experiences to feel the same degree of engagement as those around them.[58] Nothing is quite as rewarding as the pursuit of sensational, unique, intense, and stimulating experiences, and though this squirrelish nature is sometimes a source of contention, openness nonetheless drives the spirit of innovation; those who are instinctively compelled to seek out new, exciting experiences will inevitably stumble upon ideas, people, and opportunities that inspire their work.[59] Like a wriggling inner compass, the spirit of the Curious Creator is drawn in ever-shifting directions toward tantalizing experiences that others would find fearsome, but for those who prefer such nuance and change, this adventurous nature

---

[55] McCrae, R. R. (1994). Openness to experience: Expanding the boundaries of Factor V. *European Journal of Personality*, 8(4), 251-272.

[56] McCrae, R. R., & Costa Jr, P. T. (1985). Openness to experience. *Perspectives in personality*, 1, 145-172.

[57] Fayn, K., MacCann, C., Tiliopoulos, N., & Silvia, P. J. (2015). Aesthetic emotions and aesthetic people: Openness predicts sensitivity to novelty in the experiences of interest and pleasure. *Frontiers in Psychology*, 6, 1877.

[58] Roberti, J. W. (2004). A review of behavioral and biological correlates of sensation seeking. *Journal of research in personality*, 38(3), 256-279.

[59] Nicolaou, N., Shane, S., Cherkas, L., & Spector, T. D. (2009). Opportunity recognition and the tendency to be an entrepreneur: A bivariate genetics perspective. *Organizational Behavior and Human Decision Processes*, 110(2), 108-117.

can catalyze the most genius acts of creation. While the distractible, excitable tendencies of the Curious Creator may appear self-indulgent, they *must* engage this feverish side of their nature to thrive—it's essential that their buzzing energy have an outlet for expression.

The precocious spirit of the Curious Creator is really quite easy to identify: they're the child who needs an enormous amount of stimulation and creative enrichment, and while they may be labeled with an attention disorder, they're often the most gifted child in the classroom. As young adults, they're often stifled by routine and familiarity, and only come alive when they're exploring, playing, and learning something new. Indeed, the Curious Creator often self-selects into entrepreneurship because they cognitively cannot tolerate the stability and predictability of employment. The slow pace of traditional 9-5 work can feel like nothing short of *sensory deprivation* to someone who's high in openness to experience, and what's satisfying to one person may register as painfully dull to the Curious Creator. Drawn to the rush of entrepreneurship, the Curious Creator finds new venture creation to be a welcome outlet for their bursting impulses. Far from a millennial affliction, the drive to explore is a heritable personality trait believed to have been passed down from our ancestors who explored their environment and expanded their capabilities, broadening their knowledge and territory in the process.[60] For anyone who has spent time around creators, there's no questioning these explorer genes are alive and well today within the entrepreneurial spirit.

With an excitable temperament and liberal emotional expressiveness,[61] the Curious Creator is known to hop from interest to interest, but they also have a deep capacity for absorption, hypnosability, and receptivity to self-altering experiences with stimuli they find sufficiently tickling.[62] Blessed with a mile-a-minute

---

[60] Camfield, D. A. (2008). *The biological basis of openness to experience.* Swinburne U. Technology, Brain Sciences Institute.
[61] McCrae, R. R., & Sutin, A. R. (2009). Openness to experience. *Handbook of individual differences in social behavior, 15,* 257-273.

mind, their strengths tends to skew toward ideation over execution, greatly preferring creative exercises to operational work, and though they may struggle to devote their full attention to one person or project, they're brilliant multitaskers who can hold in their minds a multitude of ideas and directions. The Curious Creator may be quick to change course on strategy and vision, emotionally hooking into the most compelling thought of the moment, and while this may greatly confuse or unhinge their colleagues, it also sets them on an iterative path that reflects the true spirit of innovation. They may occasionally appear aloof or inconsiderate of the destabilizing effects of their untamed ideation and seemingly rudderless course correction, but this rapid inner processing and intense imagination can produce extraordinary outcomes when anchored by a stable team or cofounder. This behavior is rarely an office-specific quirk, and the Curious Creator's open-mindedness can also been seen in their vast assortment of hobbies, interests, friendships, and romantic relationships, as well as their appreciation for food, drink, and other sensual pleasures.[60] Indeed, the Curious Creator is more often than not the *bon vivant* of innovation.

The Dark

But uninhibited openness can transform the Curious Creator into a filterless funnel through which ideas, people, and interests come and go with little discernment, and create a reality with boundaries that are too flimsy—a phenomenon known as experiential permeability.[63] The Curious Creator may appear eccentric with a complete disregard for conventionality, and express their feelings and desires with such intensity that they are unable to distinguish between stimuli originating from inside of themselves versus their environment. This looseness of cognition can make them easily lost

---

[62] McCrae, R. R., & Costa Jr, P. T. (1985). Openness to experience. *Perspectives in personality*, 1, 145-172.

[63] Piedmont, R. L., Sherman, M. F., & Sherman, N. C. (2012). Maladaptively high and low openness: the case for experiential permeability. *Journal of personality*, 80(6), 1641-1668.

in a maelstrom of constant emotion, ideation, and interest-hopping, and the Curious Creator may be unable to settle on a strategy or set of values long enough to create with intention. They may find themselves too easily swayed by the ideas and values of investors, mentors, or aspirational thought leaders, and instead of providing a sturdy foundation from which their company can iterate with security, the Curious Creator may unintentionally create a culture that renders employees in a constant state of on-guardness, holding their breath for the next curveball. In their quest for engaging and novel stimuli, the Curious Creator's baseline for sensation may become too demanding, creating an unsustainable need for indulgence and distraction, and a relationship with work that prioritizes newness and excitement over intentional progress.

Although the Curious Creator often strives to be more focused and present, distraction may prove a constant threat to their productivity:[64] it may be painfully difficult for them to focus on operational or isolating tasks, and it's often hard for them to understand why they can be so maniacally focused on *certain* activities, but can't focus for more than a few seconds on a dull investor update. Indeed, while the Curious Creator can hyper-focus on projects that excite them, they may find themselves under-aroused and under-engaged when work demands their full attention and deep commitment. While the Curious Creator's fantastical tendencies can be frustrating to those around them, they often report that they are just as frustrated with their own flightiness, and many rightly or wrongly diagnose themselves with an attention disorder to justify this curiosity. It can be a great source of shame when the Curious Creator is accused of being selfish or fickle, especially when their adventurous distractibility is not only unintentional, but often feels out of their control. Perhaps most frustrating is that the Curious Creator's need for intense stimulation can make them feel chronically dissatisfied and disengaged with the life that's currently in front of them; they often

---

[64] Seddigh, A., Berntson, E., Platts, L. G., & Westerlund, H. (2016). Does personality have a different impact on self-rated distraction, job satisfaction, and job performance in different office types?. *PloS one, 11*(5), e0155295.

express the desire to want what they already have and simply feel *satisfied*, but struggle to find pleasure and interest in the things that seem to occupy others. In the Curious Creator's quest for stimulation, they may lose sight of the simpler things in life, like stable relationships and routine home lives, and after spending so much time in a state of high arousal, these activities can seem too humdrum and *normal*. The Curious Creator often wishes they could be content with life at a steady state, but lament that their bodies and minds won't just let them *be*.

Anecdotally, the Curious Creator often experiences tension in relationships, and tends to find themselves bored once the honeymoon phase of a romantic partnership, friendship, or work relationship is over. To stay engaged, the Curious Creator may seek out increasingly thrilling dates, exciting friends, and daring colleagues, and struggle in relationships in which the dynamic grows too predictable. In some cases, this dissatisfied tendency also plays out in their relationship with their company, and they may begin to lose interest in their once-beloved creation. The Curious Creator is often highly engaged at the start of their venture when everything is exciting and new, but may struggle to feel the same arousal once the plane is built, flying steadily, and their role is more managerial. This experience can be disheartening for both them *and* their team, and in its most extreme form, is evidenced by the Curious Creator who hops from venture to venture, unable to commit to one idea long enough to see it to fruition—often referred to as entrepreneurship addiction.[16] While the dark side of open-mindedness can appear selfish and flaky, causing many to assume the worst of intentions, this behavior is rarely malicious, and often pains the Curious Creator more than anyone else. Indeed, it's perhaps most heartbreaking when the Curious Creator begins to question the morality of their own inquisitive spirit.

To Integrate

The act of focusing, simmering down, and settling down can seem completely at odds with the Curious Creator's nature. In a way, it may feel as if it's their responsibility *not* to commit, but rather to frolic, revel, and create. And there's some truth to that: innovation is born from a desire to explore, not stagnate, and the Curious Creator's urge to play with their world must be honored to create with authenticity. Indeed, suppressed or shamed urges to explore often result in resentment, frustration, and misdirected impulses that don't benefit anyone, especially the Curious Creator. However, while creation does require newness, unpredictability, and change, it also requires stability, steadiness, and commitment. Chasing ideas without intention leaves the Curious Creator's attention aimless, and this misguided or unfocused direction can harm more than it thrills. To offer full attention and intention to their work, it's necessary for the Curious Creator to stabilize and steer the direction of their physical, mental, emotional, and spiritual energy. Without this thoughtful channeling of their inner resources, the Curious Creator may never know what it's like to design a deeply intentional life.

The Curious Creator can integrate their light and dark by welcoming opportunities for *commitment* in both life and work. Commitment is the willingness to form routines, rituals, habits, processes, and relationships that anchor one's experience of the world and support the control of one's attention. Forging commitments doesn't mean that life must become boring or redundant, but it instead moors the mind, body, and spirit so that one can play and explore with intention. In fact, many entre-preneurs experience an *abundance* of exploratory freedom once secured in a safe, consistent relationship, work environment, or home. In a career so fraught with blissful distraction, it's critical for the Curious Creator to have steady gaze points—people, places, beliefs, and rituals that instill focus, provide a grounding energy, and secure them in the present moment. This allows their creative energy to truly *land* in reality. Not only do these stabilizing behaviors help anchor the Curious Creator in the here and now, but over the long term, they can reset their baseline for stimulation, allowing them to feel more engaged with the world at a steady state. Contrary to what many believe, commitment is not the enemy of progress, but rather, it's the rooting force that anchors the creator as they ascend to ever-greater heights.

- Adopt routines, habits, and rituals that create stability (morning ritual, exercise, etc.).
- Engage in activities that are calming yet engaging (creative projects, hiking, etc.).
- Practice mindfulness meditation exercises to strengthen your attentional faculties.
- Offer your full attention to one activity (reading, conversation, etc.) before switching tasks.
- Turn your house or apartment into a *home* that feels comfortable, stable, and predictable.
- Find co-founders and employees who are intentional and thoughtful.
- Seek out friendships and romantic relationships that are engaging yet sustainable.
- Find people, places, and activities you can commit to (hobbies, friendships, cities, etc.).
- Dedicate yourself to one significant investment outside of work (pet, home renovation, etc.).
- Reflect gratefully upon your surroundings to keep your attention in the present moment.

Prompts for Deeper Self-Study

- Do you have trouble committing to people, projects, or ideas? If so, consider how you could be more mindful about selecting your energetic priorities.
- Do you struggle with restlessness and boredom? If so, consider which mindfulness practices might help you cultivate focus and calmness.
- Do you need intense physical, emotional, or mental stimuli to feel engaged? If so, consider how you could down-regulate your system to experience greater contentment in everyday life.
- Do you find that your quirkiness pushes people away from you? If so, consider how you could celebrate your idiosyncrasies in a way that doesn't distance you from others.
- Do you find that you're always the ideas person and never the execution person? If so, consider how you could act upon and follow through with your ideas.

Chapter 5:
The Sensitive Creator

The Sensitive Creator		
Dimension: Intuition	**Light Qualities**	**Dark Qualities**
• Emotional intelligence • Self-awareness • Ability to sense feelings of others • Observationality & perceptivity • Sensitivity to environment & substances • Introversion with deep relationships • Creativity & rich inner world • Ability to see patterns and trends	Instinctive; sensitive; aware; empathic; inspired; attentive; observant; independent; emotional; insightful	Ungrounded; overstimulated; overwhelmed; depleted; irrational; disconnected; isolated; reactive; drained
Motivation: To connect the dots **Mantra:** Follow your gut **Tension:** Inspiration vs. overstimulation	**To Integrate** Grounding	

A Reluctant Whale

On the surface, Will appeared to be *anything* but a sensitive soul.

I first met Will when we were assigned to co-host a charity event, and, striding in on a cloud of arrogance wearing a plaid button-up, vest, khakis, and boat shoes, I studied him with a blend of skepticism, intrigue, and, admittedly, disdain. Over the coming days, I learned that Will was a business school graduate who was known for his fraternal prowess, had one failed startup under his belt, and maintained lofty visions for his next company. As we began to work on the event together, I discovered that he lived off a diet of pizza and beer, only listened to house music, didn't own a bed frame, and spent his free time consuming exclusively sports- and startup-related content. Though I knew he was intelligent, boasting not one, but two Ivy League degrees, he acted boyishly immature when I was in the room, making clumsy cracks at my ideas and mistakes, and growing flustered whenever we had to work together. We spent several months awkwardly bobbing around each other, unsure of the reason for our shared mutual tension, and I reached the conclusion that he simply found me obnoxious. While we clearly had some strange effect on the other, I decided we were best kept on opposite sides of the table.

A few months into working together, our dynamic still hadn't improved, and he continued to make childish jabs while I defended myself with a maturity that left much to be desired. Things carried on in this way for a while, until one night at a much-needed happy hour, Will and I found ourselves in a corner, stumbling to make conversation. He must have been emboldened by several beers, because his energy suddenly turned sweet and warm, and he began to share the story of the moment he first saw me. Little did I know that Will had seen me walking out of an elevator in a coworking space that housed his last company, and it was a few weeks later that he decided to join the charity committee. Far from finding me obnoxious, he professed an intuitive knowing we were meant to be together. I was stupefied by this admission, heart beating wildly, shocked by my realization in the moment that I felt strongly about him as well. We both acknowledged the very real issues that a romantic relationship presented for our work, finding it rather humorous that everyone on the committee thought we couldn't stand each other, and while neither of us wanted to be deceptive, we kept our relationship under wraps until we could figure out exactly what *it* was.

Over the coming weeks, I learned that Will was far from the nostalgic fraternity brother I thought him to be, and was actually one of the most sublimely sensitive souls I had ever met. Will possessed a profound intuition that allowed him to know things he couldn't explain and connect the dots that were invisible to others. It took me many months to become comfortable with his uncanny intuition, as he always seemed to know exactly how I was feeling, what I was doing, and what I needed at each moment, and I was unaccustomed to, but pleasantly surprised by, such concierge emotional support. Will's intuition allowed him to be extra-ordinarily empathic, and not only did he feel his own emotions strongly, but he felt and took on my own emotions as well. With a bottomless heart that ached for the world around him, he carried packages of socks to give to the homeless on the street, adopted a kitten from a shelter to love something unconditionally, and devoted much of his energy to nonprofit work in an effort to be a part of something bigger than himself. With a patient, priestlike ear, he listened to me for hours on end, and wrote love letters that pierced my being with the sweetest potency. While it frustrated me that I was the only one who got to see the softer side of his spirit, I knew it was only a matter of time before he harnessed his gifts as an entrepreneur, humanitarian, and empath.

Beyond its moral and relational benefits, Will's intuition made him a keenly aware entrepreneurial spirit. Like a whale, he picked up on the subtlest variations in the current and could sense what was not apparent to others, like a raindrop falling into the ocean. He could gauge product-market-fit at the very early stages of a company, and could tell the outcome of a deal by the tone in someone's voice. Will's ability to intuit others' thoughts and feelings made him a truly gifted salesman, allowing him to tune in to a client's emotional state and subtly intuit his way through the trickiest of negotiations. He asked well-timed questions that drove to the heart of any matter, and with an incredible awareness of himself, others, and the world around him, he was able to create products that truly served the collective. In many ways, Will was an entrepreneurial visionary, and though he would firmly protest such accusations—rejecting any term that implied such lofty, prophetic gifts—he saw in his mind's eye the next version of reality, and when he was his best self, he made fast and decisive strides toward that vision of the future. Much to my relief, his intuition also helped him navigate a lot of the risks and blind leaps of faith he took, as he was always able to find his way through the dark, guided only by the light of his incandescent intuition.

But as a reluctant whale, Will was quick to hide his soft nature and certainly not eager to care for his sensitivities. He was *so* tapped into the world around him that he felt everything too acutely, and he often numbed his overwhelming insights and emotions with pint after pint of cheap beer. Even though he needed enormous amounts of time alone to recharge, Will was an introvert-in-denial who dragged himself to rowdy sports bars and surrounded himself with friends who did little to honor the delicacy of his wiring. Instead of offering his finely tuned body the rest and nutrition it needed, he overworked, ate sporadically, exercised in spurts, and thought the meaning of self-care was a nightcap. From a superficial perspective, I feared for his health, forcing him to take my vitamins and eat vegetables off my plate, but from a deeper, existential perspective, I also worried about the harm this was doing to his intuitive sensitivities. As I watched him bulldoze over his intuition with substances that numbed him into submission, I grew increasingly convinced that the failure of his first startup was not due to professional failings, but to the rejection of his intuitive gifts.

Unfortunately, Will had to break before he was able to accept his deeply sensitive soul. After a few too many misguided decisions and *way* too many beers, Will found himself in the depths of depression, and it was as if his spirit had taken his mind and body hostage until he could acknowledge and care for his intuitive gifts. He took this spiritual call to action very seriously, and, with an honest willingness to change, he stopped drinking, dropped his empty relationships, started meditating and exercising, and much to my delight, even purchased his own supply of vitamins. Quite unsurprisingly, once he started honoring himself, his creative world began to spring to life with abundance, work opportunities blossomed, and heart-wrenchingly beautiful poetry flowed from his pen. With eyes that grew clearer by the day, he began to revisit lifelong dreams that had gone too long dishonored, and lit up at the prospect of fully stepping into his intuitive gifts, opinions of fraternity brothers be damned. I have no idea what the future holds for Will, but I do know that he and the world will be better because he has learned to love his finely-tuned spirit.

The Light

While entrepreneurial spirits are a great many things, perhaps the most important is that they are a conduit for creation. Countless individuals carry around dreams and ideas that never see the light of day, but the Sensitive Creator channels their thoughts, feelings, and visions into a reality that can be experienced by others. In a way, the Sensitive Creator is a translation device between the ephemeral and the actual, and, as a vessel for creation, they must possess a sensitivity to something outside of themselves—a message, an energy, or some other term that suits—that infuses their being with *extra*-ordinary ideas, and offers them the wisdom to bring new creations into the world. For centuries, creators have chronicled moments of knowing, channeling, and divine inspiration, and whether or not they ascribe any religious or spiritual significance to these instances, the experience of intuition is nonetheless a phenomenon that occurs across time and culture. In Western terms, we might describe it as the ability to "skate where the puck is going," "be in the zone," "connect the dots," "follow your gut," or "read between the lines," and very often, this proclivity marks the difference between those who intuit their way to success, and those who clumsily reason their way along a most unpredictable path.

Intuition comes from the Latin *intuir*, which means "knowledge from within," and is defined as a set of nonconscious cognitive and affective processes that work in an associative, effortless, and rapid manner.[65] While terms like *intuition* or *sensitivity* may not be easily swallowed by everyone, they're nonetheless concepts that have been and continue to be researched, and are quantified by objective, physiological measures. It's now believed that entrepreneurs not only access intuition through patterns of prior experience, but through psychophysiological systems that indicate the detection of the intuitive perception of a future event.[66] The study of entrepreneurial intuition has made many researchers sound perfectly mystical, with some defining non-local intuition as a daily effort that does not involve deliberate intention, but rather comes from the heart.[67] The heart has been found to receive intuitive information before the brain, and this perception is registered by the entire electrophysiological system in the form of physiological and emotional changes.[68] The ability to access non-cognitive information is arguably the most essential blessing of the Sensitive Creator, as they must be able to find themselves in the right place at the right time with the right idea without the luxury of excessive rational analysis.[69]

While all humans are intuitive to some degree or another, it seems the individuals who embark upon the creator's journey are those who possess an *uncanny* intuition. The Sensitive Creator is often the observant child who can acutely sense their parents' emotions, and the teenager who, despite taking risks, always lands on their feet. They can easily navigate unfamiliar people, places, and situations, and have a powerful self-awareness, even if their

[65] Pigliucci, M. (2012). *Answers for Aristotle: How science and philosophy can lead us to a more meaningful life.* Basic Books.
[66] Bradley, R. T., Gillin, M., McCraty, R., & Atkinson, M. (2011). Non-local intuition in entrepreneurs and non-entrepreneurs: results of two experiments using electrophysiological measures. *International Journal of Entrepreneurship and Small Business, 12*(3), 343-372.
[67] La Pira, F., & Gillin, M. (2006). Non-local intuition and the performance of serial entrepreneurs. *International journal of entrepreneurship and small business, 3*(1), 17-35.
[68] McCraty, R., Atkinson, M. and Bradley, T. (2004) 'Electrophysiological evidence of intuition: part 1. The surprising role of the heart', *The Journal of Alternative and Complementary Medicine,* Vol. 10, No. 1, pp.133–143.
[69] Simon, H.A. (1987) 'Making management decisions: the role of intuition and emotion', *Academy of Management Executive,* Vol. 1, No. 1, pp.57–65.

peculiarities make them appear anything but self-aware. When they enter traditional workplaces, the Sensitive Creator is often able to sense outcomes before others, and this can create a great deal of tension between them and the powers that be. The Sensitive Creator is able to collect, process, and evaluate information in a more intuitive manner than managerial types,[70] and they often frustrate their superiors with conclusions that aren't born from logic, but from knowing—and these knowings frustrate superiors even more when they turn out to be correct. When trapped in the workplace, the Sensitive Creator often grows defeated that others won't let them make decisions they *know* are right, but can't explain why, and may start a company so they can honor their own inner knowings. While many entrepreneurs are wary of "flimsy" reasons for success, like intuition or chance, writing off their hunches as the result of intelligence and effort, most eventually learn that there's nothing quite as valuable as a gut feeling. This isn't to say the Sensitive Creator doesn't also rely on logic, but they recognize that some things can't be known—only sensed.

To access these intuitive nudges, the Sensitive Creator's autonomic nervous system must be particularly receptive to their environment, tuning into people and situations without prior knowledge of the end result. Any system, whether human or machine, must be finely tuned to receive and interpret messages with clarity, and the Sensitive Creator may be blessed with an especially permeable system that allows these messages in. Some individuals seem to come into the world more aware and empathic, and intuition is often, though not always, linked with the ability to pick up on the emotions of others—often referred to as being an *intuitive empath*.[71] The ability to sense emotions and create from a place of emotionality is an invaluable asset to creators, though the Sensitive Creator may hide this sensitivity under a veil of toughness and strength. While the Sensitive Creator may feel as though their

---

[70] Sánchez, J. C., Carballo, T., & Gutiérrez, A. (2011). The entrepreneur from a cognitive approach. *Psicothema, 23*(3), 433-438.
[71] Orloff, J. (2017). *The Empath's Survival Guide: Life Strategies for Sensitive People.* Sounds True.

intuitive nature is at odds with the demands of their work, they nonetheless feel the pulse of their company like their own heartbeat: just as a captain can sense a storm on a sunny day or a financier can sense a crash in a bull market, they can see patterns and trends that are invisible to others.[72] The Sensitive Creator can't always explain why a product will be the "next big thing," a pitch will fall on deaf ears, or an employee will betray them, but they just *know*, and these knowings allow them to anticipate issues, steering themselves toward people and opportunities that will lead them to success. Just as a tuning fork is a conduit for a sound vibration, the Sensitive Creator is primed and ready to receive the crucial insights that will bring their visions to life.

The Dark

But the Sensitive Creator often fails to realize that they must care for their own sensitivities if they wish to maintain their status as a conduit for creation. As the vessel through which inspiration is implanted and played out in the world, the Sensitive Creator must maintain an impeccable relationship with their mind, body, and spirit. A signal can only come through a radio if the wiring inside is intact and operating with integrity, and the same with the Sensitive Creator's intuition: if they don't care for themselves as a sensitive receiver, the message will be lost or will overwhelm the source. Indeed, the sensitivity of such intuitive and empathic individuals is both a gift and a responsibility, and the Sensitive Creator often has more substantive self-care needs than others, requiring a great deal of alone time, rest, nature, reflection, and other mindfulness practices to thrive.[73] With either a lack of awareness of their needs or an inability to honor those needs because of the demands of work, the Sensitive Creator may struggle

---

[72] La Pira, F., & Gillin, M. (2006). Non-local intuition and the performance of serial entrepreneurs. *International journal of entrepreneurship and small business, 3*(1), 17-35.
[73] Mason, R. (2005). The Energy Psychiatry of Judith Orloff, MD. *Alternative & Complementary Therapies, 11*(1), 32-36.

with their sensitivities for many years. Often, the Sensitive Creator doesn't appreciate how delicate their wiring truly is until they find themselves weathered by the elements, wondering why the message no longer sounds as clear as it once did.

In particular, the Sensitive Creator may find themselves with a highly sensitive nervous system that reacts strongly to sounds, smells, substances, and situations, from crowded networking events to drugs like caffeine and alcohol, and can quickly become overwhelmed when they sense too much.[71] They are easily inundated by the negativity or toxicity around them, and are especially susceptible to the effects of "energy vampires," often attracting colleagues, friends and partners who are narcissistic and emotionally or physically depleting. Beyond purely sensing the emotions of others, the Sensitive Creator may actually absorb those emotions, finding themselves deluged by feelings that don't belong to them. While these sensitivities provide a great deal of insight and inspiration, they may also overwhelm the Sensitive Creator or disconnect them from reality, rendering them lost in their own visions and insights. Indeed, they may operate so much in a state of potentiality that they're unable to work with those who want explanations and analysis, and this can place them at odds with investors, board members, or other key stakeholders who demand rationale behind decisions. It's a great shame when the Sensitive Creator's intuitive sight makes them appear less rigorous and devoted than they truly are.

While the Sensitive Creator requires an enormous amount of care and compassion to harness their gifts, the nature of entrepreneurial work and culture is fundamentally at odds with the demands of the intuitive spirit. From the overstimulating layout of coworking spaces to the stigma around emotionality (discussed in Chapter 11 on the Charming Creator), the entrepreneurial ecosystem does not cater to the needs of the Sensitive Creator. Because the Sensitive Creator is often unaware of how to care for their sensitivities, they may overburden their systems with the demands of work or soothe their overwhelm with alcohol, drugs, or experiences that blunt their intuitive abilities. The amount of self-care the Sensitive Creator needs to thrive is not insignificant, and they may feel guilty or fundamentally unable to give themselves the attention they need. As a leader, it may seem nearly impossible to avoid overwhelming events, negative situations, or toxic people, and many choose to ignore or hide their sensitivities, preferring burnout and depletion to self-care and compassion. It's often after an episode of burnout that the Sensitive Creator realizes the avoidance of their sensitivities is also an avoidance of their ultimate potentiality: to be a clear conduit for creation.

To Integrate

There are many metaphors for the entrepreneurial intuition—a conduit, a tuning fork, a radio—that help clarify the role of the Sensitive Creator's nervous system in the process of creation. There *must* be a systemic sensitivity to receive and perceive the messages of one's intuition, and just as entrepreneurs care for the delicate wiring of their technologies, so too must they care for their own receiver. When the conduit is blocked, ignored, or abused, any message that comes through it will be distorted, and the Sensitive Creator must learn to proudly defend their intuitive sensitivities. The act of protecting themselves from burnout and depletion is a frequent trade-off for such a finely tuned system, and it's a tradeoff that the Sensitive Creator must inevitably choose. In honoring their intuitive nature, the Sensitive Creator not only becomes a more efficient and empathic force of creative nature, but also a more astute knower and guardian of their own needs.

The Sensitive Creator can integrate their light and dark by practicing *grounding* techniques that regulate their nervous system, and help them channel the most productive insights and sensations. Grounding refers to any action that stabilizes and anchors the Sensitive Creator in their *own* mind, body, and spirit, and brings them back to the present moment when they feel overwhelmed or overstimulated. There are innumerable grounding techniques, but common examples include time in nature, warming food, drinks, and scents, breathwork, and more. Depending on whether the

Sensitive Creator is an intuitive, empath, or both, they may have different grounding needs—while all intuitives need self-care, intuitive empaths often need the most self-care to find an anchored, balanced state. The practice of grounding requires the Sensitive Creator to set firm and clear boundaries that protect their energy, emotions, time, and space, which is a difficult but necessary effort if they wish to tap into the abundance of insights that are readily available to them. Importantly, the Sensitive Creator should never feel any shame around caring for their needs—similar to the way a fine car requires quality fuel or a delicate circuit board demands a begloved touch, the systems with the most sensitive wiring must be cared for impeccably. And the entrepreneurial spirit is no exception.

- Find an office that feels calm and grounded (avoid open or loud working spaces).
- Practice exercises that bring you into your body (like yoga, dancing, tai chi, etc).
- Take time every day to close your eyes, breathe, reflect, or meditate.
- Avoid employees, colleagues, or partners who drain your energy.
- Spend time in nature and walk barefoot on the earth (called earthing).
- Consume plenty of water and spend time in and around water (bath, pool, lake, beach, etc.).
- Eat warm, nutritious food, avoiding wheat, sugar, alcohol, caffeine, and other stimulants.
- Spend time around animals and consider adopting a home and/or office pet.
- Introduce grounding elements to your space like wood, plants, earthy colors, etc.
- Find a calming mantra that centers and anchors you ("I am centered, I am safe.").

Prompts for Deeper Self-Study

- Do you find yourself drained in highly stimulating environments? If so, consider how you could avoid people or places that are particularly depleting.
- Are you highly sensitive to substances like caffeine, alcohol, or drugs? If so, consider decreasing or eliminating these substances.
- Do you feel others' emotions as if they are your own? If so, consider how you could protect and cleanse your personal space.
- Do your intuitive knowings distance you from purely logical thinkers? If so, consider how you could better articulate these knowings to others.
- Do you often feel overwhelmed or overstimulated? If so, consider what people, places, activities, and substances make you feel most grounded.

Recommended reading for the Sensitive Creator:
The Empath's Survival Guide: Life Strategies for Sensitive People by Judith Orloff MD

Chapter 6:
The Ambitious Creator

The Ambitious Creator		
Dimension: Achievement motivation	Light Qualities	Dark Qualities
• Tendency to master subjects • Desire to demonstrate abilities • Strong work ethic • Striving for improvement • Interest in developing competency • Determination to be successful	Driven; performative; motivated; competitive; aspiring; forceful; go-getting; diligent; expectant	Exhausted; comparative; disappointed; self-critical; unrealistic; strained; overzealous; impatient
Motivation: To work hard and win fast **Mantra:** Hustle harder **Tension:** Acceleration vs. exhaustion	**To Integrate** Patience	

An Unrelenting Ram

I didn't know what to make of Jack when we first met.

Jack was a hidden gem in a sea of LinkedIn spam. One morning after sitting down with coffee, I received a thoughtful message that expressed an interest in my work and a desire to collaborate. Wary of thinly veiled date offers disguised as professional requests, I had one eyebrow skeptically cocked as I suspiciously swiped through his profile. I immediately recognized the knowing smirk and unmistakable glint in the eyes of an entrepreneurial spirit, and as I conducted my due diligence, I was surprised to find that Jack was very Googleable: not only did he run his own venture, but he also led a team of intrapreneurs within one of the country's most respected institutions. His profile depicted an accomplished, respectably self-actualized 30-something-year-old who attended a top business school, boasted an impeccable career trajectory, and included photos of himself hiking and living his best life. While it wasn't my intention to find a dear friend and colleague that day, I immediately sensed that we had more than our work in common.

I had known many driven entrepreneurs before Jack, but I'd never met someone who was *quite* so intense. His home was decorated with whiteboards and checklists that reminded him of his goals, and he kept stacks of flashcards and journals full of scribbled intentions for his future. Even his leisure time was designed for accomplishment, complete with outcome-driven projects, mandatory exercise regimens, and outdoor hobbies that were unusually treacherous. In a candid moment, he admitted that his proudest moments usually involved suffering, and I weirdly understood what he meant. But as Jack opened up to me, he exposed a truth I wasn't expecting: though he was amazingly successful on paper, he felt like an imposter who hadn't begun to scratch the surface of his potential. While he set phenomenally high expectations for himself, in his mind, he was woefully underperforming. There was a tremendous gap between what he knew he was capable of and what he had achieved so far, and that dissonance created a tension he couldn't shake. While his apartment was filled with ski gear and outdoor apparel that made it easy to mistake him as a lackadaisical "ski bum," he was tormented by his conflicting aspirations to be both a rugged, easygoing mountain man *and* a world-class, successful innovator.

Far from the existential whimperings of a privileged white male, he genuinely wanted to live up to his potential, and as I developed a deeper friendship with Jack, it became increasingly clear how his achievement orientation had placed such a strain on his mind, body, and spirit. While Jack's quest for achievement was undoubtedly the source of his admirable success, it also made it really hard for him to be at peace with the status quo, and he found nothing more frightening than the hollow echo of stability, ease, and comfort. He was so focused on the *next* thing that he struggled to be in the present moment, and found it nearly impossible to sit down, slow down, and pay attention. Finding the notion of averageness far more terrifying than exhaustion, Jack had a masochistic work ethic that he deemed all but necessary, and often slept only a few hours each night, skipped meals, worked the equivalent of several full-time jobs, and was ever eager to pile even more onto his already full plate. He often careened from charismatic confidence into self-flagellating insecurity, comparing himself to the tormentingly accomplished friends he surrounded himself with. In an unthinking moment of reassurance, I reminded him of how enviably accomplished he already was, but as soon as the words came out of my mouth, I could tell I hit a nerve—he leaned back in his seat, looked me in the eye, and forcefully asserted that he hadn't accomplished *anything* yet.

In no small way, Jack equated self-congratulation with laziness, and wouldn't accept pats on the back for fear of losing his edge, remarking on his irresponsible behavior whenever he slept in or indulged in a bit too much wine. While Jack's intense focus made him a natural mountain climber, both literally and metaphorically, and kept him several peaks ahead of the rest, it also made him feel as if he never actually made it to a summit. He was always *almost* there, but never felt as if he was actually at the peak. It was as if he constantly climbed mountains, only to find that when he neared the top, there was another, even bigger mountain in front of him. I wanted to pluck him off the ground and give him a bird's-eye view of his success as an innovator and a human, because from my perspective, he had reached awe-inspiring heights. I couldn't help but laugh at the rich symbolism of his favorite sweatshirt, which boasted the outline of a ram on the front, wondering if he realized the significance of the sure-footed, mountain climbing creature: he *was* the unrelenting ram who climbed ever-higher and more daunting ledges, and it seemed his greatest lesson was reconciling his mountainous agility with his fear of never reaching the summit.

These days, after several years of friendship, Jack is a bit gentler on himself, reluctantly giving way to indulgent self-care and allowing himself to hit snooze a few times in the morning. While he's still learning not to compare himself to the "crazy successful guys at the bachelor party" or the "20-something entrepreneur who's so far ahead of me," I can tell he's finding more joy in the journey each day. It's inevitable that Jack will be successful; he's built for it in every sense. I know that, despite what he may think, he'll never let himself lose his edge, but I do hope he learns to love the view on the way *up* the mountain. There will always be another mountain for Jack to climb—and that's kind of the whole point—but I look forward to the day he can look back at how far he's already climbed and smile with self-assured contentment. For now, I continue to give him friendly reminders that he's not an imposter or a "lazy bum," but rather, he's the sure-footed entrepreneurial spirit I always sensed he would be.

The Light

The inner-voice that urges many to avoid the steepest slope up the mountain seems to be more of a hushed whisper within the entrepreneurial spirit. Indeed, the Ambitious Creator seems to be compelled by a different, much bolder impulse that screams *One more! Not quite! Keep going!* Much to the confusion of those around them, the Ambitious Creator often comes into the world with a sense of duty—a knowingness that they're meant to do something big, something significant, something *hard*. As if by compulsion, they're driven to scale the craggy side of the mountain, sensing they're not here to be average or to settle, and possess an ineffable knowing that their life will require them to face difficulty. There's an unmistakable pride in the Ambitious Creator's willingness to take the path of *most* resistance, and they often struggle to understand others' pursuit of simplicity and ease. They tend to find the notions of normalcy and averageness to be not only unappealing, but terrifying on a soul level, and it's often the less fearsome option to do hard things that can lead to success. For better or for worse, the Ambitious Creator feels both the energetic capability and personal responsibility to achieve greatness,[74] and there's no amount of money or fame that can outpace this ferocious, existentially-tinged motivation.

Achievement motivation is correlated with both the choice to become an entrepreneur as well as venture performance, and is a personality trait defined by its intensity, focus, mastery, and effort.[74] While many individuals desire success, the Ambitious Creator's desire for success is matched by a willingness to establish high standards for themselves and strive for constant improvement.[75] Entrepreneurship may be the rarest career in that it offers the potential to achieve seemingly unlimited heights, and this limitless ceiling on success is a most enticing fuel for the Ambitious Creator's spirit. Unlike employees whose contributions may be lost in an assembly line or managers who succeed by enabling the performance of others, the Ambitious Creator can stake an unmistakable claim over their achievements and tie their successes directly to their efforts. This visible connection between effort and progress is admittedly satisfying to the Ambitious Creator, and they often struggle to understand how employees and managers are motivated to do work that's not *theirs*, rejecting roles in which their achievements are limited or not credited back to their own efforts. This is why the Ambitious Creator will work doggedly hard starting

---

[74] Collins, C. J., Hanges, P. J., & Locke, E. A. (2004). The relationship of achievement motivation to entrepreneurial behavior: A meta-analysis. *Human performance*, 17(1), 95-117.

[75] Sajilan, S., Hadi, N. U., & Tehseen, S. (2015). Impact of entrepreneur's demographic characteristics and personal characteristics on firm's performance under the mediating role of entrepreneur orientation. *Review of integrative business and economics research*, 4(2), 36.

their own company, yet seem all but incapable of completing the most basic functions of their former jobs.

From a young age, the Ambitious Creator is marked by one or more unmistakable qualities: they have a desire to achieve mastery, avoid failure, demonstrate their abilities, and avoid appearing incompetant.[76] While the child or teenager who grows into the Ambitious Creator may not always channel their achievement motivation into schoolwork, they invariably find some kind of "side hustle" that allows them to prove their worth in a way that's uniquely satisfying to them. As they grow older, the Ambitious Creator often finds themselves wincing at job descriptions, corporate hierarchy, and glass ceilings, and may view entrepreneurship as a way to tie their achievements back to their own tireless effort. While many are quick to judge the Ambitious Creator's achievement-motivation—crediting ego, greed, pride, and the like—the need for achievement has deep cultural and genetic roots, and is believed to be genetically wired into our nation's DNA as a country of immigrants who bear all of the essential qualities of entrepreneurs: immigrants are driven to work hard, make sacrifices to achieve their dreams, and create better lives for future generations.[17] This concentrated energy of achievement may in fact be why work ethic is so glamorized in the United States—concepts like "hustle" and "grind," as damaging as they might be, nonetheless motivate the Ambitious Creator with the notion that if they work hard enough, they can achieve the dream that they feel to be their birthright.

If the Ambitious Creator's work ethic comes under scrutiny, it's generally due to excessive drive, not lack thereof. Achievement motivation is significantly correlated with both the choice of an entrepreneurial career as well as entrepreneurial performance,[74] and reflects an intense, prolonged, and repeated attempt at something

---

[76] Elliot, A. J., & Harackiewicz, J. M. (1996). Approach and avoidance achievement goals and intrinsic motivation: A mediational analysis. *Journal of personality and social psychology*, 70(3), 461.

that would make others wilt. The idea of pursuing something intense and difficult is often a strangely appealing notion for the Ambitious Creator who *prefers* tasks that require effort, skill, risk, and difficulty,[77] and they're usually uninterested in pursuing something or someone if it doesn't feel like a challenge. To remain engaged and interested, the Ambitious Creator must feel expanded, not contained by the activity, which is a cause for both celebration and frustration. The Ambitious Creator sets high expectations for their work, ever willing to put in the effort to achieve those goals, and often expects the same from those around them. Unlike those who talk about big dreams but never act upon them, the Ambitious Creator savors nothing more than execution, completion, and progress, and even after the most strenuous feats of labor and love, they can't help but set their sights on the next great peak to scale.

The Dark

But not all forms of achievement motivation are adaptive, *especially* the kind that has permeated the entrepreneurial ecosystem. Today's entrepreneurial culture boasts a near-maniacal focus on other-worldly achievements and hustling one's way to success,[78] and whether it's size, status, or logos adorning pitch decks, it seems that even the most remarkable achievements are no longer worthy of note. The media has rightly compared American entrepreneurship to a modern-day religion in which the Ambitious Creator is expected to adhere to a brutal, puritanical work ethic, but love their lashings regardless. In what often looks like a fraternal hazing process, entrepreneurial culture tends to consider sleepless nights and desks strewn with empty coffee cups a rite of passage, and has arguably stigmatized self-care more than burnout. Look no further

---

[77] McClelland, D. C. (2010). *The achieving society.* Martino Publishing: Mansfield Centre.
[78] Vaynerchuk, G., & Vaynerchuk, G. (2017). *Hustle: The Cure For Those Who Complain.* Retrieved from https://www.garyvaynerchuk.com/hustle-cure-complain/.

than the inspiration porn littering social media and coworking mantras that urge them to "love the struggle," "crush it," and "hustle harder" to see how normalized the notions of moonshots, money, and massive success have become. While this celebration of achievement is often intended to inspire the Ambitious Creator, cheering them on along an admittedly difficult path, it more often does just the opposite: when the Ambitious Creator is placed in a culture that pornographically glorifies achievement—particularly hyper-masculinized achievement—a combustive extreme is all but guaranteed.

The hustle and grind culture of entrepreneurship can exacerbate the Ambitious Creator's adaptive achievement motivation, and transform it into a maladaptive drive to overwork and overachieve, often resulting in disappointment and other deleterious effects on well-being.[79] The Ambitious Creator may find themselves chronically dissatisfied with their own achievements—setting goals for themselves that are self-flagellating at best—and fail to celebrate the milestones they *do* reach. In an effort to keep up with the breakneck pace of innovation, the Ambitious Creator often selects idols and mentors who have achieved otherworldly success, yet ignores the personal sacrifices—the strained relationships, health issues, and the like—these individuals have made to achieve such success. Particularly in today's ecosystem rife with "30 under 30" lists, meaningless accolades, and gratuitous celebrations of personal achievement, it's all too easy for the Ambitious Creator to feel as though they are falling behind, forcing them to maintain an exhausting front of resilience, competitiveness, and relentless effort.

Quite cruelly, the Ambitious Creator may find that, once they taste success, they're still not satisfied, and feel as though they're "imposters" who don't have the skills to compete with those around them. This experience—referred to as imposter syndrome—affects

---

[79] Elliot, A. J., & Sheldon, K. M. (1997). Avoidance achievement motivation: a personal goals analysis. *Journal of personality and social psychology, 73*(1), 171.

even the most intelligent and accomplished of creators, and is defined as a psychological pattern in which individuals think their accomplishments are insufficient, and are fearful of being exposed as a fraud.[80] The pillars of entrepreneurship have been poorly constructed with no end goal in sight, and when the Ambitious Creator compares themselves to today's unicorns, it's all too easy to feel like an imposter with insufficient skills or intelligence. In the most extreme cases, the unrelenting need to achieve may result in hyper-aggressiveness, ruthlessness, and a temptation to push harder, cut corners, and disregard stakeholders,[81] and un-surprisingly, the entrepreneurial spirit doesn't *truly* thrive under these extreme pressures. As a result of this masturbatory relation-ship with achievement, the Ambitious Creator often burns out in mind, body, and spirit, leaving them to sit with the false assumption that their peers are more resilient than they. While there's a great amount of pleasure to be found in achievement, there's no nobility to be found in the self-abuse that's so prolific in today's entre-preneurial ecosystem.

To Integrate

The willingness of the entrepreneurial spirit to stand in front of a mountain and see an opportunity is something we must collectively applaud. It's because of the Ambitious Creator's tolerance for challenge and discomfort, and desire for achievement and success that our society benefits from creations that require unfathomable amounts of toil and tears. But in the game of new venture creation, entrepreneurs must often go slow to go fast, and without the ability to appreciate their accomplishments along the way, many will continue to experience the plight of the hungry ghost—creatures with large, empty stomachs and pinhole mouths who starve for a

---

[80] Sherman, R. O. (2013). Imposter syndrome: When you feel like you're faking it. *Am Nurse Today*, 8(5), 57-8.
[81] Miller, D. (2014). A Downside to the Entrepreneurial Personality? *Entrepreneur-ship Theory and Practice*, 39(1), 1–8.

nourishment that will never arrive.[82] The Ambitious Creator often pushes back when they're encouraged to release their attachment to hustling, insisting they love the grind, and these protests should be met with great empathy. Working hard, no matter the costs, comforts the Ambitious Creator with the notion that they're doing all they can to ensure an otherwise uncertain outcome. But the truth is that the Ambitious Creator does *not* need to be pushed harder, and if anything must be reminded to slow down and be softer with themselves. While an unlimited ceiling can be empowering, a ceiling that's *too* high can also be ironically claustrophobic, making the Ambitious Creator feel as though success is only ever achieved by someone else.

The Ambitious Creator can integrate their light and dark by strengthening their capacity for *patience* with themselves, their company, and their aspirations. Patience is the capacity to tolerate delay without suffering, and is characterized by understanding, gentleness, and leniency. With a patient mindset, the Ambitious Creator gives themselves permission to make slow progress toward achievable goals, knowing that success will arrive in its own time. While patience may seem like a counterintuitive practice in the innovation landscape, there are few if any examples of overnight successes, and it often surprises the Ambitious Creator that deepening their capacity for patience tends to quicken the pace with which successes arrive. With patience inevitably comes a kinder inner-dialogue and looser attachment to outcomes, and the Ambitious Creator is often astonished by the gifts this relaxed perspective brings. While some creators may be tempted to do the exact opposite—surrounding themselves with people and activities that drive them ever harder—most will eventually realize that degree of patience they show themselves is a surprisingly good predictor of the success they will achieve. In the natural world, everything is accomplished at a slow to medium pace, and for the Ambitious

---

[82] O'Brien, B. "Hungry Ghosts of Buddhism - Definition." *Learn Religions*, Learn Religions, 8 Jan. 2018, https://www.learnreligions.com/hungry-ghosts-449825.

Creator, psychologically sustainable creation will likely come from adopting the pace of nature whose secret is patience.[83]

- Advise yourself as you'd advise a child—with patience, compassion, and softness.
- Set realistic goals and expectations for yourself, your employees, and your company.
- Reflect upon what success really means to you (family, love, comfort, belonging, purpose).
- Avoid exposure to gratuitous celebrations of entrepreneurial success.
- Create a company culture that avoids the glamorization of "hustling" or "grinding."
- Build self-care rituals into your schedule for proper rest, nutrition, and exercise.
- Allow the abundance of nature to recharge you (fresh food and water, beauty of nature).
- Set the example for your company around taking vacation, not emailing on weekends, etc.
- Make a regular practice of celebrating small successes and embracing failure.
- Spend time with people who give well-earned praise and encourage you to care for yourself.

Prompts for Deeper Self-Study

- Do you compare yourself to others? If so, consider what your *personal* metrics of success look like.
- Do you skip meals, sleep, or exercise to get work done? If so, consider how you could carve out sacred time to protect these acts of self-care.

---

[83] The Complete Works of Ralph Waldo Emerson. (2007). *Choice Reviews Online*, 44(12).

- Do you feel as though you are an imposter? If so, consider all of the reasons that you have earned your successes.
- Do you set unrealistic goals for yourself and your work? If so, consider how you could set more compassionate goals.
- Do you worry that you're falling behind? If so, consider the notion that your progress is happening in its own perfect time.

Chapter 7:
The Disruptive Creator

The Disruptive Creator		
Dimension: Disagreeability	**Light Qualities**	**Dark Qualities**
• Willingness to risk social disapproval • Tendency to be confrontational • Critical-mindedness • Bluntness to the point of harshness • Unwillingness to cooperate and follow rules • Desire to challenge the status quo	Assertive; critical; blunt; innovative; stubborn; change-oriented; willful; feisty; headstrong; skeptical; free-thinking	Antagonistic; judgmental; unkind; defiant; loner; discontent; distant; combative; uncooperative; suspicious
Motivation: To challenge assumptions **Mantra:** Disrupt the status quo **Tension:** Innovation vs. destruction	**To Integrate** Gratitude	

A Cranky Donkey

Eric was the sweetest curmudgeon I'd ever known.

The founder of a Baltimore-based startup, there was no networking event or awards list that was complete without Eric's presence. While he often graced the cover of the city's who's-who magazines that wagged their tongues at his success in business, I befriended him for quite another reason: despite the fact that he received the affection of many, he didn't care much for the approval of others.

With a sharp eye and tongue to match, he was charmingly disagreeable, and, much to the dismay of stakeholders and investors, was interested in few others' opinions but his own. A most stubborn human, Eric was willing to risk bent rules and bruised feelings in the name of innovation, and said exactly what he thought, tact and grace aside. He seemed fundamentally unable to mince words, frequently finding himself with his foot in his mouth, and while his efficient candor was at times affronting, it nonetheless made me feel as if I always knew where I stood with him. I found his disagreeable nature to be surprisingly refreshing, and his blend of boyishness and bullishness to be endearing, and though we became fast friends, I secretly hoped he would be gentle when it came to our blossoming friendship. One of my top love languages has always been words of affirmation, and I perhaps naively believed that I would be able to avoid the disagreeable protests of this cranky donkey.

The first time I visited his home for a dinner party, the space was exactly what I expected from such a discerning soul: it was a stunning, all white apartment with not a hair out of place, and he didn't even have trash cans in the bathroom lest it distract from the intentionally spartan aesthetic. I held my breath as he gave me the tour, wondering what he would think of my colorful apartment with knickknacks and stacks of books cozily cluttering the surfaces. But nonetheless, I appreciated Eric because he knew what he did and didn't like, and designed his life the way he designed his company—*exactly* as he pleased. A blend of eternal optimist and cutting pessimist, his disagreeable mind made him a tremendous entrepreneur, allowing him to pick apart the world so he could spot flaws and opportunities, and correct issues before they turned into catastrophes. When others declared something as "good enough," he stubbornly pushed for excellence, and with pungent opinions that gave his products an enviable level of integrity, he built an intentional business with a clear mission and brand. With a build-first, apologize-later mentality, his rejection of others' opinions allowed him to create innovative products that most only appreciated *after* they were built, and there was so much value in his disagreeable persona that his employees, partners, and investors reluctantly tolerated his breed of ornery genius.

In a sincere effort to improve the world and its inhabitants, Eric took on the responsibility of letting people know how they or their product could be improved upon, even if his opinion was woefully unsolicited. If anything was ever so slightly amiss, he dutifully and loudly hee-hawed in protest, and this naturally made every outing a cringeworthy and cartoonish escapade. When we went to group dinners, he wouldn't be seated unless we were at the table with the exact right ambiance, and once a suitable seat was secured, his big brown eyes darted around the room as he rattled off all of the different issues with the venue. He often made these criticisms known to the waiters, waitresses, and owners, and all I could do was hold my breath, curl my toes, and pray for it to be over. Such protests, as comedic as they were blush-worthy, became the stuff of our everyday friendship: I was thrilled the day he sent me birthday flowers, but he was not as pleased, scowling in protest at their "garish" colors. On a vacation with friends, he booked a pricey room in a five-star hotel, and spent 36 hours criticizing the views, service, and "cheap" chocolate on the pillows. Indeed, Eric was willing to buck against anything and anyone if the outcome was an improved version of reality.

It was clear that Eric simply wanted to help people and products overcome the gap between their current reality and fullest potential, and he was ready to risk hurt feelings if it meant inciting those around him into action. In fact, Eric's willingness to express and act on his observations was at the heart of his innovative personality, and he was an effective entrepreneur because of, not despite, his deadpan focus on disrupting the status quo. But while I first saw his disagreeable personality as a charming quirk, I was less pleased when he began directing his pokes and prods at *me*. If I said red, he said maroon. If I said warm, he said sweltering. If I said yes, he said, "yes … but." Whether it was the scent of my dryer sheets or the color palette of my outfits, everything I did was met with swift and sharp, though usually accurate, analysis. While I knew that Eric wanted me to be the best version of myself, never intending to hurt my admittedly sensitive feelings, our friendship was an ironic misalignment of my top love language. But as much as his rearing defiance hurt me, I could tell it hurt him more: he lived in a world in which there was *always* something wrong, and it was as if he was constantly in a fight with his surroundings. There was always a bone to pick and a complaint to lodge. His keen perception made him anxiously aware of every flaw, while his inability to fix problems made him depressed, and for many years he struggled to cope with the harsh clarity with which he saw his world.

But after years of depleting negativity and overstepped fine lines, Eric has learned to tolerate the burdens of the world with a bit more grace. We've remained close friends over the years, and I've watched him fondly as he's devoted himself to mindfulness practices that temper his critical mind and cool down his oft-hot head. I'm happy to share that these days, he's a far more pleasant spirit who has taken the edge off his disagreeability through meditation, intro-spection, spiritual practices, and a relationship with a grounded partner who doesn't tolerate his button pushing. Eric now navigates a world in which there's more *right* than wrong, and is ever-willing to point out when he himself is the one in need of improvement. He is now just as devoted to innovating himself as he is the world around him, and exudes more and more lightness every time I see him, wielding his critical mind with admirable and perfectly imperfect effort. And it pleases me to share that, after all these years, I can finally communicate with him using my favorite love language: words of long-awaited, heartwarming affirmation.

The Light

The entrepreneurial spirit is a beautiful, complex force—but that doesn't mean it's always a joy to work with. The Disruptive Creator often freely admits that they've always been rather disagreeable and mulishly stubborn, and most wouldn't have it any other way. Innovation isn't born from a contentment with the world as it is, but from a willingness to push into discomfort to birth something new, to compete rather than cooperate.[84] Those who are committed to a life of innovation must be willing to shine a light on the flaws that others would prefer to ignore, even and perhaps especially if a few feathers are ruffled in the process. While our culture often shames the Disruptive Creator for their noncompliant, obstinate moments—the cursing rants, cutting criticisms, and colorful acts of rebellion—this disagreeability also gives rise to the *disruptive* personality that is celebrated with equal fervor. Indeed, disruption could be argued to be the antithesis of agreeability—it requires a contrarian nature that challenges the status quo and is willing to disquiet the minds of others. Disruption and agreeability rarely exist in harmony, and entrepreneurs *must* have some willingness to be disagreeable if they wish to create something truly innovative.[85] While many would prefer to avoid conflict and criticism, the Disruptive Creator understands that a purely agreeable attitude is incongruous with the requirements for successful creation.

Entrepreneurs are significantly less agreeable than non-entrepreneurs,[86] and this personality trait manifests as a willingness to break from the status quo in an outspoken if not uninhibitedly quarrelsome manner.[87] The disagreeable personality is happy to bend rules, contradict ideas, and challenge the powers that be, and, interestingly, agreeability is *negatively* related to status, earnings, and creative accomplishment.[88] While agreeability is characterized by traits like cooperativeness, generosity, and tolerance,[89] the

---

[84] Costa, P. T., & Mccrae, R. R. (1992). The Revised NEO Personality Inventory (NEO-PI-R). *The SAGE Handbook of Personality Theory and Assessment: Volume 2 – Personality Measurement and Testing*, 179–198.

[85] Gladwell, M. (2013). *David and Goliath: Underdogs, misfits, and the art of battling giants*. Hachette UK.

[86] Zhao, H. & S.E. Seibert. (2006). The big five personality dimensions and entrepreneurial status: A metaanalytical review. *Journal of Applied Psychology, 91*, 259-271.

[87] Patterson, F. (2002). Great minds don't think alike? Person-level predictors of innovation at work. *International review of industrial and organizational psychology, 17*, 115-144.

[88] Nettle, D. (2006). The evolution of personality variation in humans and other animals. *American Psychologist, 61*(6), 622.

[89] Digman, J. (1990). Personality structure: Emergence of the five-factor model. *Annual Review of Psychology, 41*, 417–440

disagreeable personality is more likely to make tough decisions that cause short-term pain for long-term payoff. In no small way, the stomach for this discomfort places the Disruptive Creator at an enviable advantage: freed from the constraints of social niceties, they spend much less time people pleasing and much more time executing, and are willing to tolerate rejection, confrontation, and isolation in the stubborn pursuit of what they think is right.[90] It often seems that the Disruptive Creator is driven by the energy of conflict and tension, relishing nothing more than a hard left when others turn right, but when harnessed properly, this insubordination is the stuff of disinhibited creation. With just enough scrappy disobedience, the Disruptive Creator can forge new realities with true authenticity, unencumbered by the rules and norms that inhibit so many from reaching their full potential.

The young spirit who grows into the Disruptive Creator is often a handful from the moment they become verbal. They can be identified at a young age through their willful stubbornness, debates with teachers and playmates, and schoolyard troublemaking, and as they grow older, they are often fierce protagonists of the powers that be and quick to break rules that don't resonate. When it comes time to secure a job, the Disruptive Creator often finds the world of employment rather unwelcoming of their "move fast and break things" mentality, and realizes that traditional offices are largely designed for the agreeable souls among us. The structure of organizational settings requires employees to defer to those above them, and the Disruptive Creator often finds it counterproductive, if not entirely offensive, to wait for approval, ask permission, and follow corporate playbooks. Frequently found arguing with superiors and stubbornly asking "why" in response to every request, those who aren't cut out for deference leave employment—by choice or necessity—and embark on the journey of entrepreneurship. Many times, the Disruptive Creator never even attempts to find a full-

---

[90] Bègue, L., Beauvois, J. L., Courbet, D., Oberlé, D., Lepage, J., & Duke, A. A. (2015). Personality Predicts Obedience in a Milgram Paradigm. *Journal of Personality*, 83(3), 299-306.

time job, knowing they'd rather have no job than be forced to play by someone else's rules, as there's nothing more smothering to their spirit than the pressure to conform. Indeed, the Disruptive Creator has an all-too-real understanding of the protest: *give me liberty or give me death.*

While the Disruptive Creator may at times test the patience of those around them, they nonetheless possess the assertiveness to keep them one step ahead of the competition after the niceties are exhausted. The Disruptive Creator's tolerance of rejection and adversity allows for more efficient creation, and there's an enviable amount of resilience to be found in the willingness to risk social disapproval; the ability to feel secure in one's worth outside of group approval is invaluable when one's goal is to create something that has never existed before.[91] Unconcerned with outside validation, the Disruptive Creator is freed to truly think creatively, and with a disregard for rules and structure, this expansive mindset breeds the genius of the innovative persona. While they may be slow to trust or show affection, the Disruptive Creator is less likely to allow the concerns of others to interfere with decision making, and their willingness to share their thoughts, even if it leaves others red-faced and flustered, allows them to give fast feedback when it's needed most. This radical transparency can at times come across as a lack of social graces and empathy, but it's rarely intended as cruel criticism: the Disruptive Creator often feels a sincere compulsion to improve the world around them, and their honest feedback is shared in the name of progress. Although the delivery can often leave much to be desired, their intentions are usually noble.

The Dark

There's a mighty fine line between disagreeability and depleting negativity, and, when left unrestrained, the Disruptive Creator may

---

[91] Graziano, W. G., & Eisenberg, N. (1997). Agreeableness: A dimension of personality. In *Handbook of personality psychology* (pp. 795-824). Academic Press.

find themselves at constant odds with their world. Many struggle with a contradictory tension between their optimistic and naysaying nature, flipping from eagerly enthusiastic to cuttingly negative with breakneck unpredictability. While disagreeability can be an invaluable quality, the Disruptive Creator may find it impossible to turn off their critical, fault-finding reflex, making them feel as though their reality is filled with incompetent people, terrible ideas, and faulty products. There's a fine line between criticism and judgment, and the Disruptive Creator often finds themselves less than constructive in their opinions, constantly tripping over faux pas and too-harsh truths.[92] Charged with a feisty compulsion to innovate, the Disruptive Creator may feel entirely stifled if they're not doing something to change or improve the world around them, not realizing that in the process, they're prioritizing destructive disruption over intentional productivity. Indeed, the Disruptive Creator's oft-disrespectful approach to disruption feeds into the stereotype of the naughty, feisty, or even tyrannical entrepreneur.

Much to the aggravation of co-founders, employees, and romantic partners alike, the Disruptive Creator often experiences significant relational obstacles.[93] They themselves are often confused as to why they pick big and small fights with individuals they have no desire to hurt, but nonetheless feel an impulsive urge to defy, and it often seems as though they're trying to create conflict for the sake of tension. They may wonder why others take their constructive criticism or defiant actions so personally, especially because it's often the Disruptive Creator's deepest desire to help others meet their potentialities, and they tend to impose the high expectations they have for themselves on those around them in the spirit of tough love. The Disruptive Creator is often quite aware of their button-pushing effect, setting deliberate intentions to operate with a bit more tact and empathy, and may find themselves frustrated when they instinctively revert to harshness and skepticism. They're

---

[92] Jensen-Campbell, L. A., & Graziano, W. G. (2001). Agreeableness as a moderator of interpersonal conflict. *Journal of personality*, 69(2), 323-362.
[93] Shackelford, T. K., Besser, A., & Goetz, A. T. (2008). Personality, marital satisfaction, and probability of marital infidelity. *Individual differences research*, 6(1).

often troubled by their inability to trust and accept others, especially when those around them seem to easily soften into the status quo and be at peace with the world in which they live. Perhaps the most heartbreaking result of disagreeability is the isolation that comes from living in a reality in which there's always something wrong.

It's important to note that while disagreeability is often nothing more than an irksome trait, it occasionally has more serious manifestations. When taken to an extreme, disagreeability can result in pathological rule breaking and the complete disregard for the opinions of others, leaving the Disruptive Creator in a deviant, aberrant, or un-equivocally toxic way of being.[94] While some entrepreneurs are indeed Machiavellian in nature and are the ones often villainized by the media for their brash actions and cold demeanor, this is the exception rather than the rule: for the most part, the Disruptive Creator has not a hint of cruelty in their spirit. It's also important to note the differing levels of criticism placed on disagreeable male versus female entrepreneurs. Female entrepreneurs are judged ever more harshly for their disagreeable temperaments,[95] and it's crucial that no gender distinctions are made in moral judgments of disagreeability. As a consequence of this double standard, many female entrepreneurs ascribe to either extreme agreeability or extreme disagreeability, feeling they need complete social approval or disregard for social approval to reach their goals. But in the end, neither of these strategies is a sustainable approach to innovation, and it often takes many years for the Disruptive Creator to realize that creation requires the effort of not one, but many.

To Integrate

If the Disruptive Creator is accused of being a curmudgeon, it's almost certainly born from their genuine desire to improve the

---

[94] Spain, S. M., Harms, P., & LeBreton, J. M. (2014). The dark side of personality at work. *Journal of organizational behavior*, 35(S1), S41-S60.
[95] Judge, T. A., Livingston, B. A., & Hurst, C. (2012). Do nice guys—and gals—really finish last? The joint effects of sex and agreeableness on income. *Journal of personality and social psychology*, 102(2), 390.

world, maximize the potential in everyone and everything, and protect their creation from harm. We cannot celebrate innovation and condemn the Disruptive Creator, as disagreeability is a prerequisite for progress. But while the disagreeability of the Disruptive Creator is a driver of innovation, there comes a time on their journey when they must soften into the vulnerable underbelly of life and work, including its imperfections and annoyances, its rules and niceties. It can be exhausting to constantly create against the grain and buck at the powers that be, and without the ability to choose their battles discerningly, energetic depletion is all but guaranteed. Like a governor that limits the top speed of a vehicle, the Disruptive Creator must find practices that act as a governor on their disagreeability, tempering its intensity while honoring its battle cries for willful stubbornness, intentional protest, and productive rule-breaking. When complemented by tact and reverence, disagreeability can be a most productive fuel on the fire of creation.

The Disruptive Creator can integrate their light and dark by cultivating *gratitude* for people and products in their current—albeit likely flawed—state. Gratitude is the ability to feel contentment, express thankfulness, and experience awe. When innovating, it's essential to show gratitude for the traditions, long- held beliefs, or past efforts that have gone into the product or service that is now ready to evolve. Irreverent or destructive disruption is rarely well-received, and when the Disruptive Creator maintains a stance of gratitude, they find that they can disrupt the status quo while honoring what already exists. Far from a trite self-help exercise, cultivating gratitude teaches the Disruptive Creator to appreciate what exists, and be mindful of the impact of their innovative impulses. The most simple thoughts, words, or actions of gratitude have the power to transform a conversation, relationship, or entire company culture, and a nod or a word of praise can make the difference between contentious and collaborative energy. Gratitude does not necessitate a false sense of agreeability—in fact, many individuals and environments that practice gratitude are also constructively critical and righteously rebellious. While the

Disruptive Creator should never iron over their feistiness to fit in, they must also cultivate their capacity for respectful innovation, grateful for all the creators who came before them.

- Carve out space to praise your employees, partners, and cofounders (meetings, emails, etc.).
- Share positive feedback before delivering negative feedback.
- Invite others to collaborate in areas of your work that are currently solo endeavors.
- Start each morning with a gratitude reflection practice (journaling, meditation, etc.).
- Reframe judgmental thoughts to focus on the positive aspects of a person or situation.
- Meditate on the embodied sensation of gratitude, respect, awe, and appreciation.
- Create a regular gratitude practice inspired by nature (gratitude for abundance, seasons, etc.).
- Calm irritable urges with a steady breathing technique (box breathing, etc.).
- Spend time doing activities and in environments that inspire awe (concerts, sunsets, etc.).
- Use conversational techniques, like "yes and…" that foster a collaborative conversation.

Prompts for Deeper Self-Study

- Do you need to do things differently than everyone else? If so, consider how you could be more collaborative in your endeavors.
- Do you frequently find yourself in confrontations? If so, consider how you could engage in interactions with greater empathy and respect.
- Do you spot the flaws in everyone and everything? If so, consider how you could interact with the world with greater acceptance.

- Do you find yourself disagreeing for disagreements sake? If so, consider how you could experience more appreciation in your daily life.
- Does your desire to break with the status quo often backfire? If so, consider how you could be disruptive in a more amenable way.

Chapter 8:
The Empowered Creator

The Empowered Creator		
Dimension: Ego	Light Qualities	Dark Qualities
• Confidence in one's abilities • Feelings of self-worth and respect • Positive beliefs and emotions about oneself • High resilience and adaptability • Sense of authentic personal power • Motivation to achieve and to win • Ability to be responsible and accountable	Self-assured, confident; impactful; responsible; resilient; effective; accountable; leader; commanding; proud	Selfish; arrogant; vain; grandiose; domineering; prideful; delusional; insecure; defensive; validation-seeking; condescending
Motivation: To claim power **Mantra:** I am worthy **Tension:** Assurance vs. arrogance	To Integrate Values	

A Well-Fluffed Peacock

I met Ally a few years ago at a dinner party in New York City.

It was a loud, rambunctious evening, and everyone had consumed just enough red wine to initiate the triadic ritual of networking, socializing, and flirting. The dimly lit loft flickered with a sea of candles as New York's most notable entrepreneurs and venture capitalists mixed and mingled about. It was the largest gathering of entrepreneurs I'd ever been to, and my barely of-age self watched mesmerized as the most self-assured beings bounced from partner to partner, navigating the bodies in the room like an effortlessly coordinated dance. The whole space buzzed with an electricity that was all too palpable, and I found it nearly impossible to sit down and focus on my increasingly cold entree. I was new to the startup space at the time, and, knowing almost none of the attendees, I scanned the room in search of a friendly face. Out of the corner of my eye, I spotted a smartly dressed woman with long, wavy hair and an undeniable *je ne sais quoi*. There was something about her energy that intrigued every fiber of my being and so, taking another sip of wine, I grabbed my clutch, smoothed my dress, and walked over in search of a new friend.

Little did I know, this mystery woman was one of the Big Apple's most successful entrepreneurs. Ally was the city's latest tech luminary who emanated an irresistible energy of confidence, and with charisma, lady swagger, and an impeccably tailored persona, you just *knew* that anything she touched would inevitably turn to outsized returns. Idolized by women, desired by men, and envied by anyone with a hint of an entrepreneurial spirit, Ally was an easy celebrity among New York's tech scene. She just had that *thing*. As I asked other attendees about this enigmatic force, they gushed over how big of a deal it was that she was here, and in no small way, the whole room acted strangely deferential toward Ally, as if we were in the presence of royalty. With a massively successful startup and a presence that spoke for itself, she was a catch for venture capitalists and single New Yorkers alike, and that night, everyone wanted to steal a moment of Ally's time. While I always assumed entrepreneurship to be rather democratic, I would learn that night that there exists a powerful, unspoken hierarchy.

Like a well-fluffed peacock, Ally sat confident and proud as if a halo of captivating feathers cocooned her seat. No one was immune to her pulsing personal power, and she radiated an energy that was at once self-assured and aloof—if she was the moon, then everyone else was the tide adjusting and bobbing around her. She was clearly aware of the effect of her magnetic essence, and she chose to dole it out in selective, minuscule droplets to those thirsty for her attention. Perhaps it was my own ego that wanted to test my influence over the moon that evening, and I tried everything in my power to draw her attention. After weaving and bobbing my way into a chair next to Ally, I was prepared to commence our friendship. But much to my dismay, my quippy remarks were no match for her fabulous feathers. Ally made me feel as if she saw *right* through me, perhaps with the intention of peering at the attractive man behind me. I retreated with a bruised ego, soothing myself with the notion that she was probably a jerk.

After that night, I saw Ally everywhere—on panels, podcasts, and power-posing on the cover of tech magazines with her boss-lady outfits and perfect sound bite responses. I was fascinated by the way she wielded her power as a successful woman and observed her clear delight as she was bathed in the spotlight that celebrated her brains, beauty, and comfortably padded ego. Following her sudden launch to fame, the media was quick to latch onto her story of prodigal success, and though she seemed to relish the attention and power that came with her rise to fame, I couldn't help but wonder who was running her company while she managed her teeming press schedule. But interestingly, as her company continued to climb ever-higher, there came a day when she disappeared from my news suggestions and social media feed, and eventually, it seemed she had fallen off the map completely. Out of curiosity, I checked to see if she was still running the company, and indeed she was. Without thinking too much about it, I assumed Ally's star had risen and fallen out of view, and the world turned its attention toward the next founder of the week.

It would be six years before I met Ally again. In a moment of perfect serendipity, we were both invited to the same conference, and as I sat down in a front row seat for the keynote talk, I saw her breeze through the crowd and land on the chair next to me. I couldn't help but giggle to myself, *Is the moon now coming to the tide?* At first, Ally didn't recognize me, but I instantly recognized her. In fact, I didn't even have to look to know it was her, as I could just *sense* that familiar, metallic tang of confidence. As she turned to introduce herself, I held my breath, wondering if she would remember our encounter from many moons ago, when suddenly, the light of recognition spread across her face. But this time, she was different—*very* different. With feathers more humbly displayed, the wall that had once existed between her and everyone else was gone, and she exuded a much gentler, softer presence. With open body language and engaged eye contact, Ally showed genuine interest in my work and was warm in our brief rendezvous before the speaker took the stage. I couldn't help but smile through the keynote because I could tell, based on the two data points I had on her, that she was now an objectively happier person.

I once again found myself captivated by Ally, but this time, I wasn't drawn to her confidence, but to her humility. I learned that a combination of time, experience, and marriage had taken the edge off Ally's ego, and a few public stumbles had quickly nudged her ego into place. Ally shared that she had replaced the vanity of entrepreneurship with service projects, empowered perspectives, and candid vulnerability, and intentionally extricated herself from the media circus that was once a central part of her role as a tech founder. Like a hollywood celebrity grown weary of the paparazzi, she told me that she largely avoids the spotlight, unless it's to promote a social or philanthropic cause, and has realized what a shallow source of validation such attention can truly be. Upon learning that she too had a passion for entrepreneurial well-being, I shared more about the book I was writing, eager to hear her two-cents. She grew roused and curious, and without missing a beat she said, "Don't forget to include a chapter on ego and narcissism." So here we are.

The Light

The Empowered Creator is wired with an ineffable sense of worth—an underlying foundation of self-belief that, even when challenged, is the sturdy pride that fuels their journey. In a way, the Empowered Creator's confidence seems different from everyday confidence: it's not just an internal esteem, but a projection of power that imparts change and inspiration on the world around them. Sometimes it seems this esteemed stance is not so much a skill or a mindset as it is an *energy*, and it often comes across as an electric force that others can feel from across a room. The Empowered Creator's golden worthiness is likely the reason they are so often followed, envied, and admired, as a strong ego is not only productive, but *magnetic*. It's hard not to believe in someone who believes so sincerely in themselves, and the Empowered Creator may be easy to follow because they comfort others with the notion that they're expansive enough to hold the enormous responsibility that is creation.

Unsurprisingly, the ego—often measured as a composite of qualities like self-assurance, courage, and desire to take charge—is a core character theme that defines entrepreneurs.[96] Without these feelings of competence and inherent worth, most would simply crumble under the pressures of new venture creation. That said, it's important to clarify the nature of the Empowered Creator's ego, a concept that has taken quite a beating from the entrepreneurial community as of late. With the rise of Stoicism and other traditions that criticize the ego, it's easy to assume that all feelings of self-worth are naughty, especially in the wake of the media's breathless chronicles of self-destructive, egotistical founders whose narcissistic personalities were the reason for both their rise and downfall. These egoic entrepreneurs are often portrayed as a new class of super-villain, and while the entrepreneurial ecosystem has understandably been burned by the idea of ego, a strong and healthy ego is a *crucial* part of the human psyche.[97] The word ego is Greek for "core sense of self," and the ego acts as a self-consciousness system that supports an individual's identity, goals, and desire to ensure their own survival, without which they'd have no attachment to their own existence. There is a difference, however, between a weak, unhealthy ego and a strong, healthy ego: someone with a weak ego will have interests that are selfish, insecure, and shallow, while someone with

---

[96] Thompson, J. L. (2004). The facets of the entrepreneur: identifying entrepreneurial potential. *Management decision*, 42(2), 243-258.
[97] Henriques, G (2013). The Elements of Ego Functioning. *Psychology Today*.

a strong ego will be characterized by generosity, security, and impact.[98]

The Empowered Creator often comes into the world bearing a strange kind of burden. It's as if they *know* they are meant to stand rooted in their power, lead with intention, and use their confidence as a buoy that others can latch onto in moments of doubt. It's often described by entrepreneurs as an unmistakable glint of knowing-ness, or a feeling of being "chosen" or "special" ever since they were little. But far from a self-important specialness, the Empowered Creator senses early on that they're meant to carve out a unique path and create something *big* with their lives. It's a specialness that fills these quirkily self-assured children with feelings of power and capability to pursue grand dreams that most leave in their child-hood bedrooms. Once they enter the workplace, the Empowered Creator is often feared by the powers that be, and there tends to be comically overt power struggles between them and their superiors. Drawn to the agency, autonomy, and accountability of entre-preneurship, the Empowered Creator with high entrepreneurial drive can use their business as a means to achieve self-esteem,[99] and their sturdy self-esteem to support their bold endeavors—it's a flywheel empowerment phenomenon.

A strong ego is essential for the Empowered Creator, as without it, the potential to build something of recognized value is wasted.[100] The Empowered Creator is noticeably *anchored* in their being, exuding a palpable sense of self-assurance, responsibility, account-ability, and courage,[101] and they are largely driven by their need for independence and desire to make a difference.[102] This sturdy ego

---

[98] Staik, A (2017). Ego Versus Ego-Strength: The Characteristics of a Healthy Ego and Why It's Essential to Your Happiness. *PsychCentral.*

[99] Carland Jr, J. W., Carland, J. A. C., & Carland III, J. W. T. (1995). Self-actualiza-tion: The zenith of entrepreneurship. *Journal of Small Business Strategy*, 6(1), 53-66.

[100] Maritz, A. (2005). Entrepreneurial orientation in a franchise system. In *Proceedings of the 4th International Business and Economy Conference, Hawaii, January.*

[101] Bolton, W., & Thompson, J. L. (2003). *The entrepreneur in focus achieve your potential.* London: Thomson.

[102] Bolton, W., & Thompson, J. (2004). *Entrepreneurs: talent, temperament, technique.* Amsterdam: Elsevier/Butterworth-Heinemann.

doesn't go unnoticed by others, and the Empowered Creator naturally gravitates to positions of leadership in which their internal locus of control offers them the courage to confront situations, face reality, and stand rooted in their beliefs.[100] The Empowered Creator is solid enough in their intrinsic worth that they can face failure without compromising the respect they have for themselves, and this empowers them to run toward challenges without the promise of accolades, awards, or certain success.[98] With the ability to create from a solid sense of self, the Empowered Creator presents themselves with authenticity and intention, and they tend to be beloved—even if occasionally feared—leaders. Perhaps the reason they are feared is because the Empowered Creator is willing to take complete responsibility and accountability for their own actions,[100] a quality that only the sturdiest leaders possess.

The Dark

While a healthy ego is an entrepreneurial asset, many creators struggle with the integrity of their ego over their careers. Indeed, the entrepreneurial path is paved with tests that challenge the health of the ego, and as the Empowered Creator begins to receive the unexpected gifts of entrepreneurship like praise, validation, money, and even celebrity, the *unhealthy* or *weak* ego can develop. Recognizable by its narcissistic qualities, an unhealthy ego is characterized by grandiosity, inflated self-views, vanity, entitlement, low empathy, and exploitative behaviors.[103] An unhealthy ego often develops after the Empowered Creator's power is reflected back to them in an undeniable way, like after they raise a large sum of money, receive a coveted award, claim power over another group of people as a boss or thought leader, or some other situation that places them in a position of precedence. Seemingly overnight, the Empowered Creator finds that their thoughts and feelings are

---

[103] Campbell, W. K., Hoffman, B. J., Campbell, S. M., & Marchisio, G. (2011). Narcissism in organizational contexts. *Human resource management review, 21*(4), 268-284.

treated as more valuable than others, and are shown how much influence they can truly wield. The more the Empowered Creator claims this superiority, the more they tend to be externally rewarded, and the more their ego comes to rely on this weak source of nourishment.

The Empowered Creator may come across as self-opinionated and arrogant, and the extreme ego has been argued to be one of the most difficult facets of the entrepreneurial persona to cope with.[100] As the Empowered Creator struggles with the health of their ego, they may begin to reject friends, activities, and values they once viewed as fundamental in favor or people and situations that validate their ego, and become uncharacteristically preoccupied with external metrics of success, like press attention and attractive investor logos on pitch decks. They may start attending events or activities that imply a certain level of exclusivity, and to the great confusion of those around them, may regress from humble founder who's willing to take out the trash into an entitled leader who's above mundane tasks. Importantly, an extreme ego in an entrepreneurial leader may directly conflict with their ability to lead a team, and there may be power struggles between the leader's independence and the team's priorities.[100] The emotions of the Empowered Creator may become increasingly volatile, swinging from high to low in line with their latest success or failure, and their work often becomes increasingly characterized by the showboating and peacocking, rather than actual execution. Indeed, it seems there's often a direct, inverse correlation between the Empowered Creator's *actual* successes and their effort to *showcase* their success.

All of this said, it's a mistake to vilify the Empowered Creator—even in the thick of ego-driven tendencies. While the media is quick to judge the ego-driven entrepreneur, they're also quick to celebrate and indulge the ego, and the rise in egoism is believed to be a product of our current entrepreneurial ecosystem that glorifies superficial uniqueness: we tend to praise the appearance of self-esteem over the cultivation of genuine self-esteem. The Empowered Creator who develops egoistic tendencies is rarely dark or sadistic, but instead has found a mirror in which their self-worth is reflected.

Indeed, narcissistic behavior stems from a combination of two drives we *all* share—the drive for survival and the drive for self-esteem[104]—and the Empowered Creator uses their work as a means to build and sustain those feelings of esteem.[48] But while entrepreneurship can be a potent reminder of the Empowered Creator's authentic power and worth, it can also offer unhealthy validation and fleeting reflections of their value. This is why the Empowered Creator often aggressively protects their work and status, and can come across as jealous and secretive: they are trying to maintain control over a seductive reflection of personal worth.

To Integrate

One of the most interesting things about the entrepreneurial ego is that the Empowered Creator is so often *aware* of their ego—they dislike its weighty mandates and seek to mitigate its sway over their life and work. This in and of itself should comfort the Empowered Creator with the realization that they're not pathologically self-interested, but rather a worthy spirit who's being tested to balance their power and influence with humility. The Empowered Creator with an inflated ego almost never has malicious intent, and instead seeks validation for the daunting journey they've chosen. There's no shame in accidentally crossing the line between a healthy and unhealthy ego, and for the Empowered Creator who learns from experience, they often *must* dance with the ego's demands before they learn to keep it in a state of integrity. While there's usually no single grand slaying of the ego, there *is* usually an incident or series of incidents that begin to humble the Empowered Creator. Whether it's a failure, the birth of a child, or some other event that thrusts them into a state of heightened humility, selflessness, or vulnerability, the Empowered Creator often learns through a series

---

[104] Maccoby, M. (2017). Waking up in this Age of Anxiety NAAP Speech 11:18. Retrieved from http://www.maccoby.com/PDFs/Waking_Up_in_This_Age_of_Anxiety_NAAP_Speech_111817.pdf.

of challenges that their sense of worthiness will come from creating something that's of service for the collective.

The Empowered Creator can integrate their light and dark by claiming a set of *values* to guide their life and work. Values reflect an individual's anchoring philosophy that unifies their sense of self, and prioritizes how they spend their energy and make decisions. If we look at the Empowered Creator who truly embodies a healthy self-esteem and a grounded sense of authentic power, they're almost always driven by a core set of principles that create a snug alignment between their work and their beliefs. By placing questions like ethics and morality at the forefront, the Empowered Creator learns the value of servant leadership, and measures success not by attention, but by impact. After a joust with the unhealthy ego, the Empowered Creator often finds great peace and dignity in the backseat, and there may be a sense of relief when they realize they don't need to play the egoic games that are so pervasive in the entrepreneurial ecosystem. Entrepreneurship likely always will be a tempting game of seduction and validation—after all, creating something from nothing based on one's own vision is an admittedly self-centered exercise. But when the Empowered Creator creates a constitution of their values, they can find their way back to a humble center. Again and again and again.

- Reflect upon the ways your work has had an impact on your sense of worth.
- Make a list of the entrepreneurs who embody healthy self-esteem.
- Take stock of the external sources of validation you rely on (social media, clubs, awards, etc.).
- Consider what you will find valuable in 10 years, in 20 years, at the end of your life.
- Spend time with friends, family members, and colleagues who accept you without conditions.
- Reflect on the core values you have for your life and work.
- Create a mantra, phrase, or word that reconnects you with your core values.

- Rethink what successes you share publicly and why you're sharing them.
- Avoid the people or situations that artificially or temporarily inflate your self-esteem.
- Consider how you can present yourself and visions more humbly.

Prompts for Deeper Self-Study

- Do you crave outsized fame or success? If so, consider why you feel the need for such significant measures of success.
- Do you come across as arrogant? If so, consider how you could present yourself more humbly while maintaining self-respect.
- Do you always think you know best? If so, consider how you could incorporate the opinions of others into your life and work.
- Do you need to be in a position of power? If so, consider where this desire for power stems from.
- Do you feel the need to have others witness your success (awards, lists, etc.)? If so, consider the validity of your work without this external recognition.

Chapter 9:
The Fiery Creator

The Fiery Creator		
Dimension: Passion • Increased motivation and drive • Positive emotions like pride and love • Willingness to take initiative • Enhanced mental activity and creativity • Feelings of meaning and importance • Willingness to explore risky opportunities • Preference for passion over reason	**Light Qualities**	**Dark Qualities**
	Devoted; impassioned; intense; absorbed; embodied; engrossed; committed; steadfast	Obsessed; consumed; dysregulated; self-sacrificing; crazed; unconditional; blinded; feverish; delirious
Motivation: To be energized **Mantra:** Live your passion **Tension:** Devotion vs. obsession	**To Integrate** Boundaries	

A Caged Tiger

Olivia was a founder who bled the blood of passion.

When I first met Olivia, her attention had never been more in demand. As one of the most successful founders on the East Coast, it was notoriously hard to steal a minute of her time, and the senior colleagues at my company were a bit resentful that she responded to my emails faster than anyone else's. Over several months, Olivia and I developed a friendly rapport over email, and, drawn to her endearing cheekiness, I happily accepted when she invited me out for a happy hour drink. I immediately recognized her green eyes and blond hair waiting for me at the bar, and after a first meeting that was far more personal than professional, I began to understand why she had risen to such heights: she had an intense tigerlike energy, a penetrating gaze, and a passion that could transform dirt into sparkling potential. Even though Olivia had a reputation for being a bit rough around the edges, she was wise beyond her years and gave off a seasoned grittiness like a young soldier who made it through a war. Her fiery love for her work radiated from her being with a contagious force, and before long, I too found myself fascinated by this tiger. I figured people who were so passionate about their work must be equally passionate in their friendships, and I was pleasantly surprised to learn I wasn't wrong.

Olivia was the founder of a well-known startup that was being acquired for many, many millions of dollars. She started her company fresh out of college, and rose to startup fame during some of the most formative years of her life. By her mid-twenties, she was already known as a force within the entrepreneurial ecosystem, and her name was littered across every podcast, panel, and 30-under-30 list in town. Like a young parent, she devoted a decade of her early adult years to her fledgling company and wove her identity directly into her work. During a life stage in which her friends were buying homes, climbing corporate ladders, and finding partners, she was wedded to her company, and much to the dismay of her romantic partners, her work was never not top of mind. While she made a great many sacrifices to start her company, she thought of herself as a martyr for a worthy cause, and her work in turn sustained her: it not only made her a local celebrity, but offered her enviable feelings of energy, excitement, and *passion*. With a tribe of employees who were equally devoted to the cause, they spent 10 years in the trenches together learning, growing, failing, and channeling their passionate energy into something that made a difference. They truly felt as if they had been through a battle and not only survived, but conquered.

I met Olivia as she was navigating the acquisition process, and the outcome appeared to be everything she could have wanted. From the money to the attention to the cushy executive role at the well-known acquiring company, it seemed like the ultimate endgame. This was the outcome she had worked so hard for, and Olivia dreamed of the satisfaction that would come from the acquisition, certain it would provide her with the long-awaited freedom to sit back, have a glass of wine, and reflect on her well-earned success. She made a plan, albeit stereotypical, for her "early retirement," and decided to leave her home on the East Coast for a mountain house on the founder-laden slopes of Park City, Utah. She imagined her life as a wise sage living on a mountaintop, armed with mala beads and a new meditation practice, doling out advice to aspiring entrepreneurs and finding long-awaited inner stillness. Olivia was ready to unwind from a decade of nonstop, dogged hard work and just *be*.

But much to her dismay, the post-acquisition glow didn't sit with her as naturally as she had hoped. One night, while I was on the road for work, I received a call from Olivia in the midst of an existential quandary. She had just finished a day of snowboarding, and was making her way back home when she saw two ski bums sitting on a bench. The scene was everything she thought her new life *should* be. They seemed blissfully content with nothing to do, no one to impress, and no next venture coming up the pike. There were no VCs or lawyers to answer to, and no pinging, buzzing, beeping phones in their gloved hands. The ski bums embodied everything Olivia wanted at this stage of her life: they seemed relaxed, present, and unconditionally content. And yet, as I listened to Olivia, it was obvious that *her* contentment was nowhere to be found. She felt a stirring, buzzing energy that was trapped inside of her and now had no outlet for release, and it seemed as though she'd been rendered completely useless. Without her comrades, battle duties, and full inbox to defeat, she felt she had lost the whole plot of her life. She had become a martyr without a cause.

From the outside looking in, it appeared as though Olivia had reached her endgame. She started something from nothing, built it into an empire, and was positioned to indulge in the spoils of war. But as it turned out, Olivia's freedom was more fidgety than fun. She had spent so much time in the "on" position that her gears had become frozen, and she didn't know how to turn herself off. The past decade had been so focused on the *next* product feature, *next* city launch, *next* funding round, or *next* award that she didn't know how to displace the energy that was once consumed by her passion. She had grown so accustomed to the satisfaction of meeting goals, deadlines, budgets, and expectations that she didn't know how to feel excited in her new life as a ski bum. Without her company, her passionate energy had no purpose, and she began to feel crushing pangs of guilt and anxiety without something to *do*. She needed to be needed, and even though everyone else saw her as a unicorn, she was crawling out of her skin. And on the quiet, dark nights in Park City, her discontent mounted like the snowbanks outside her window.

Olivia taught me that you can take the founder out of the mission, but you can't take the mission out of the founder. She had lost the outlet through which she converted her energy into impact, and with it came a crisis of passion. The company that had sustained her energy, emotions, and identity for a decade was now in the hands of someone else, and she didn't know what to do if she wasn't sacrificing herself for the good of her work. While it wasn't easy for Olivia to find peace after years of embodying the blazing passion of a founder, it also forced her to introduce a new dynamic into her relationship with her work—*balance*. She learned that she could never be so reliant on work for her emotions, energy, and identity, and that she'd be better off in the long run if she diversified her investment of passion into other endeavors. While entrepreneurship will always be a passion for Olivia—it's her gift and her lesson to master—she's also learned to be passionate about her role as a partner, sister, explorer, student, spiritual seeker, and occasional troublemaker. More and more, I see a wholeness radiating from her as she carves out a path of true and sustainable passion—one that's more of a slow, steady burn than an incendiary furnace. To this day, we're still dear friends, and I smile with fondness as I type these words and think of her sitting on a bench next to those ski bums. I imagine her leaning back with a soft smile on her face, feeling a sense of total contentment exactly where she is, in the rich fullness of simply being herself.

The Light

Passion is perhaps the most overused word in entrepreneurship, which is quite a statement in a space that has notoriously made trite many words in the English language. With slogans like "live your passion" plastered across the halls of coworking spaces and covers of tech magazines, the concept of passion has become so deeply diluted that many have lost touch with what it means to truly be *passionate*. But despite the casual and often irreverent use of the term, passion is nonetheless at the heart of entrepreneurship, and is said to be the most observed phenomenon in the entrepreneurial experience.[21] While it may seem like a flimsy or trendy concept, the Fiery Creator's passion offers them energy and positive emotions needed to persist against all odds, and creates a fierce identification with their work that's binding on a professional and, one could argue, existential level.[105] While the Fiery Creator is in some ways similar to the Ambitious Creator (achievement motivation) and the Existential Creator (self-actualization), there are a few key distinctions. If achievement is the left-brained quest for success, then passion is the right-brained quest for excitement. If self-actualization refers to the greater *why* of our existence, then passion refers to the emotions and energy that fuel the pursuit of meaning.

The Fiery Creator often speaks about their work with no less fervor and quivering intensity than a religious prophet or political revolutionary, and it has been argued that entrepreneurial passion is born from the same genes as spiritual and political leaders.[17] There's something almost supernatural about a job that requires one to create something from nothing, and entrepreneurial work is often quite miraculous in its ability to materialize what was

---

[105] Murnieks, C. Y., Mosakowski, E., & Cardon, M. S. (2014). Pathways of passion: Identity centrality, passion, and behavior among entrepreneurs. *Journal of Management*, 40(6), 1583-1606.

previously a mere ideal. The impulse to embody one's passion to such an extreme—to make it one's work, life, identity, and ritual offering—is one that few are wired with, but the Fiery Creator exhibits all but instinctively. For the Fiery Creator, the decision to make tremendous personal, financial, and reputational sacrifices seems parentally instinctive, and they intuitively engage with their work as if it's not so much a job but a *duty*, not so much a career but a *contribution*. This is perhaps why entrepreneurship is met with such ardent fascination by today's popular culture: the passion of the Fiery Creator comforts the masses like a modern-day savior, promising to save humanity from all sorts of disorder, disease, and boredom. This isn't meant to glorify creators, but there is a sanctimonious view of entrepreneurship that imbues founders with a savior-like quality, and the Fiery Creator chooses to take this existential responsibility *very* seriously.

Passion is perhaps the surest giveaway of a young person who will ultimately become a creator, and the Fiery Creator is characterized by a blazing, feisty energy that *needs* to be channeled into something outside themselves. They often feel incomplete without something to wholeheartedly throw themselves into, and many angstily fidget through their teenage years and early adult life until they find something that's a worthy recipient of their all-consuming energy and emotions. Like a tiger pacing around its cage, the Fiery Creator is filled with an intense desire to pounce, but is often maddened by the constraints of their age, resources, or awareness of *what* to do with their passion. Passionate energy can be all-consuming, and, if not given an outlet for expression, it can feel like nothing short of soul-crushing suffocation. When cooped up in schools and offices, the Fiery Creator often finds themselves frustratingly, and sometimes destructively, bouncing off the walls in an earnest attempt to find identity-relevant and emotionally important work, and may redirect their passionate energy into romances, hobbies, or troublemaking until they find a fitting outlet. They often stumble across their passion through a hobby, side job, or offshoot of their work that feels autotelic—it does not require external praise or reward because it is satisfying in and of itself.[106] When the Fiery Creator aligns with their passion—when they embody it and experience its energy, emotions, and existential urgency—it's a sensation they can't readily unknow.

Correlated with everything from tenacity to initiative to increased likelihood of receiving funding,[107] the Fiery Creator's passion is a contagious energy that directly affects those around them, like employees, co-founders, and potential investors.[108] To be worthy of the Fiery Creator's passion, the activity must be one they like or love, and provide identity-relevant goals that help them form their sense of self.[21] Indeed, the Fiery Creator often defines themselves in complete alignment with their work, and is motivated to succeed because of their work's inextricable connection to their internal self-concept and external reputation:[109] they don't just love technology—they *are* a technologist. They're not just good at marketing—they *are* a marketer. They didn't just found a company—they *are* a founder. While the tendency to identify with one's work has been exacerbated by our culture of self-marketing that emphasizes what one does rather than who one is, a strong identification with one's work is essential for the Fiery Creator. Far from a trendy millennial mindset, the Fiery Creator's work *must* be deeply meaningful to their self-concept, as this identity salience provides a motivating and heartfelt attachment between them and their creation—it's incredible what the Fiery Creator can accomplish when their sense of self relies on it. This powerful identification with their work creates a readiness to tolerate discomfort, risk, uncertainty, and financial strain, and a willingness to make reasonable sacrifices to ensure the survival of their creation.

---

[106] Csikszentmihalyi, M. (1997). *Finding flow: The psychology of engagement with everyday life.* Basic Books.

[107] Cardon, M. S., Sudek, R., & Mitteness, C. (2009). The impact of perceived entrepreneurial passion on angel investing. *Frontiers of entrepreneurship research,* 29(2), 1.

[108] Cardon, M. S. (2008). Is passion contagious? The transference of entrepreneurial passion to employees. *Human resource management review,* 18(2), 77-86.

[109] Cardon, M. S., Wincent, J., Singh, J., & Drnovsek, M. (2009). The nature and experience of entrepreneurial passion. *Academy of management Review,* 34(3), 511-532.

When harnessed fully, the passion of the Fiery Creator transforms mere-mortal tasks into a prayer-like act of devotion.

The Dark

But when blinded by the heat of passion, it's all too easy for the Fiery Creator to take their devotion to an inflammatory extreme. Indeed, there are two kinds of entrepreneurial passion—harmonious and obsessive—and the difference between the two is similar to the healthy or unhealthy attachment to any other addictive substance or behavior. While the harmoniously passionate entrepreneur engages in work they find important and has the ability to disengage at will, the obsessively passionate entrepreneur has a controlled internalization of the activity in their identity that makes them feel as though they *must* engage in it[110]—they're not only devoted to their work, they're a blinded martyr. The Fiery Creator in the grips of obsessive passion may find themselves in a controlled relationship with work, feeling as though work is something they must do: they *have* to go into the office or *must* reply on a weekend, and much to the frustration of friends and romantic partners, they often experience guilt and anxiety when they're not working. The embodied experience of passion can create a very real sense of longing when separated, and the Fiery Creator often feels both negative emotions and a literal *aching* when forced to detach from their work.

Like a lover swept up in a fit of passion, the Fiery Creator doesn't know what they would do or who they would be without their passion, and they're often frustrated that they can't experience similar levels of engagement in other activities, like hobbies or relationships. Addiction to or obsession with one's work may feel quite a lot like an obsessive romantic relationship, and the dopamine-motivated Fiery Creator may exhibit addictive patterns

---

[110] Fisher, R., Merlot, E., & Johnson, L. W. (2018). The obsessive and harmonious nature of entrepreneurial passion. *International Journal of Entrepreneurial Behavior & Research*, 24(1), 22-40.

in both work and life. These addictive tendencies—whether to work, a partner, or a substance—involve the brain's dopaminergic "reward system," and evoke states like craving, euphoria, tolerance, and intrusive thinking.[111] In this addicted state, the Fiery Creator may be distracted in day-to-day life until they can engage with their work once again, and find that they are no longer in control of their passion, but rather, their passion controls them. The Fiery Creator may think that if they're *not* obsessed, they're doing something wrong, and it seems there are few entrepreneurial role models who aren't blindly obsessed with their work. Indeed, the concepts of sacrifice and commitment have become so glamorized that it's no wonder entrepreneurs struggle to find the healthy boundaries of passion. For the Fiery Creator lost in the throes of passion, they may feel damned if they do and damneder if they don't.

While it may seem as if the Fiery Creator can't have too much passion, it's apt to note that the word passion comes from the Latin *passio* for suffering, and passion has historically induced many self-immolating acts that harm both the individual and the object of their passion.[109] Though these passionate gestures and emotional displays may seem nobly righteous in the moment, there's little glory in self-sacrifice and martyrdom, and the Fiery Creator may find themselves overworking, overcommitting, and overgiving in the name of passion. Obsessive passion is a fast path to entrepreneurial burnout,[112] a condition characterized by emotional exhaustion, depersonalization, and a reduced sense of personal accomplishment,[113] and this state of distress may give a whole new meaning to the concept of *burning passion*. Of course, the Fiery Creator who's obsessively passionate is a deeply dedicated soul

---

[111] Fisher, H. E., Xu, X., Aron, A., & Brown, L. L. (2016). Intense, passionate, romantic love: a natural addiction? How the fields that investigate romance and substance abuse can inform each other. *Frontiers in psychology*, 7, 687.

[112] Shepherd, C. D., Marchisio, G., Morrish, S. C., Deacon, J. H., & Miles, M. P. (2010). Entrepreneurial burnout: Exploring antecedents, dimensions and outcomes. *Journal of research in marketing and entrepreneurship*, 12(1), 71-79.

[113] Maslach, C., Jackson, S. E., Leiter, M. P., Schaufeli, W. B., & Schwab, R. L. (1986). *Maslach burnout inventory* (Vol. 21, pp. 3463-3464). Palo Alto, CA: Consulting psychologists press.

whose only fault is loving a thing too much, and it's unfair to celebrate and condemn them for the same tendency. Entrepreneurship makes disorientingly dissonant demands of the Fiery Creator to be both passionate and impartial, making an impossible suggestion that they should give of themselves entirely, yet not burn out in the process.

To Integrate

The Fiery Creator *must* have an outlet to channel their passionate energy, and often only feel half alive when they're not creating. There's no shame in the Fiery Creator's desire to do things wholly and intensely, and their brilliance comes from their willingness to throw themselves into their work. The Fiery Creator *wants* to be devoted, *wants* to be turned inside out, and *wants* to be so invested that their lives are filled with intensity and love. Indeed, it's almost a romantic notion that creators can be so unconditionally committed to their creations, and slow-burning passion carries many entrepreneurs through the trials and tribulations of entrepreneurship. It's not unusual for the Fiery Creator to dive in and out of obsession throughout their career, and one could argue that they *must* experience obsessive passion to learn the importance of creating with harmony. Often, the Fiery Creator is only compelled to confront their obsessive passion after they've grown personally, professional, or financially depleted, and there's no shame in hitting the lows of professional martyrdom in order to learn— creators are experiential learners, and most will only make a change after they have no other option.

The Fiery Creator can integrate their light and dark by establishing *boundaries* that help them engage with life, work, and relationships with greater intentionality. Setting boundaries entails a willingness to create guideposts around how much the Fiery Creator will give of themselves. A boundary can be thought of as an invisible line that separates the Fiery Creator from everything else, and it's up to them to decide *where* those boundaries are and *how* they will react when they're crossed. While boundaries may seem like an unappealing if not entirely misguided notion to the Fiery Creator, suggesting that they shouldn't be completely invested in their work, they are nonetheless a necessary precaution. Passion, like fire, is both a creative catalyst and a destructive force, and the Fiery Creator must understand what they are and are not willing to sacrifice to the flames of passion. It takes intention and mindfulness to declare how devoted one is willing to be, how much time, money, or energy one is willing to sacrifice, or what relationships, hobbies, or experiences one is willing to forgo in the name of work. But for the Fiery Creator, it is essential that they firmly declare their limits and defend their most valuable resources: their time, emotions, identity, and, of course, their precious energy.

- Find co-founders and employees who balance your passionate energy with objectivity.
- Use the breath, gentle movement, and the element of water to cool any fiery tendencies.
- Reflect upon the important aspects of your identity outside of work (sister, yogi, etc.).
- Set clear financial boundaries to determine how much investment is appropriate.
- Spend time engaging in nonwork activities that create a state of absorption and flow.
- Use meditation and reflection exercises to break obsessive thoughts about work.
- Write down people, activities, or interests you won't sacrifice for work (children, running, etc.)
- Channel unused passionate energy into exercise, relationships, and creative projects.
- Create reminders to stop, rest, and recharge your body during long work sprints.
- Calm your impassioned emotions with a coach, therapist, or mindfulness practitioner.

Prompts for Deeper Self-Study

- Do you often martyr yourself (overgive, overdo, overspend, etc) for your work? If so, consider how you might set healthier boundaries.
- Do you only feel energized when you're working? If so, consider other activities that might make you feel similarly alive.
- Do you feel guilty or anxious when you're not working? If so, consider how you might cultivate a less anxious relationship with work.
- Is your identity inseparable from your work? If so, consider how you might broaden your identity into other domains.
- Is your mood dependent on the status of your work? If so, consider how you might develop a more consistent internal environment for yourself.

Chapter 10:
The Orderly Creator

The Orderly Creator		
Dimension: Conscientiousness • Strong self-discipline • Orderly processes • Reliability for important tasks • Industrious work ethic • Thorough deliverables • Attentiveness to detail • Desire to control outcomes **Motivation:** To create order **Mantra:** Control your destiny **Tension:** Organization vs. perfectionism	**Light Qualities**	**Dark Qualities**
	Attentive; organized; cautious; impeccable; deliberate; watchful; regimented; discriminating	Controlling; perfectionistic; anxious; hypervigilant; militant; compulsive; neurotic; fussy; untrusting
	To Integrate Trust	

A Fussy Bee

Nick was a bit ... nit-picky.

The founder of a small, local tech startup, Nick was his calmest, most productive self when everything was *just so*. While he had all the qualities of a visionary, he was most impressive in his role as an operator and knew exactly how each and every widget of his life was supposed to work. Like a fussy bee, he constructed his hive with a perfectionist's touch, and, much to the admiration and frustration of those around him, wouldn't settle for anything less than an impeccable product. After several years in a corporate role in which Nick had no control over anything, he saw entrepreneurship as a lifestyle in which he could be the master of his own universe—he could organize his life and work to his satisfaction, and nudge every last detail to his liking. When I first met Nick, I marveled at his orderliness and diligence, though I was certain there was no way a relationship between us could work. I was the crumb-maker, and he was the crumb-cleaner, and we would surely drive each other mad within a matter of meals. But strangely enough, this contrast created a snug, humorous bond between us in which he learned to love my knotty hair, and I learned to love his buzzy, fussy energy. Together, we learned a great many lessons, with Nick learning to tolerate disorder, and me learning to make my bed properly.

But Nick's tolerance for disorder only went so far, so to manage the chaos of his startup, he created spreadsheets. Countless spreadsheets with carefully cultivated pipelines and processes, precisely manicured rows, and color-coding for days. It didn't surprise me when, one afternoon, Nick called me into his office for a surprise, and I leaned over his shoulder to see a Google Spreadsheet glowing on his screen. With a pride that was both naive and endearing, he puffed his chest as he walked me through a new spreadsheet for his company with bottomless customer funnels. With its clean lines and properly executed spreadsheet functions, he acted as though the most innovative feat of engineering wouldn't have been a more notable accomplishment. As Nick unveiled his surprise, I ceremoniously cooed and cawed, marveling at his organizational triumph with wide-eyed fawning and admiration. I wasn't being disingenuous, but rather, I knew how much he wanted me to celebrate his efforts, and he was so sweetly pleased with himself that I was happy to accommodate. After dating him for several months, I had become quite well-practiced in this routine.

But as he closed the customer pipeline, his screen revealed another spreadsheet that immediately caught my eye—it was titled "Jess Metrics." We both froze in a moment of palpable awkwardness, as I heard several expletives run through his mind. A jolt of nervous energy rushed up my spine as my pupils dilated with intense vigilance, and I quickly scanned the screen to soak up its contents before he clicked away. It was at once the most romantic and cringeworthy thing I had ever seen: his "Jess Metrics" spreadsheet tracked our relationship with unbelievable precision, including a Likert scale of how happy he made me, a reminder to send me a morning love email, a tracker of how many times he made me laugh, a log of our dates, and a counter of how many days had lapsed since our last "incident." It was a perfect manifestation of Nick's quirky breed of conscientiousness, and it was so authentically bizarre that I couldn't help but savor the sweetness of it, like the funniest kind of honey.

Over the coming months, I learned that Nick's detail orientation didn't stop with work and relationships. He tracked every mile he ran, beer he drank, and dollar he spent, and any habit he adopted, however mindful, was performed with ritualistic rigidity. With 12 plaid shirts that hung pressed and motionless in his closet, his spartan studio apartment contained exactly one bed frame, one end table, one faux fur rug, one stack of books, and one cat, and Nick's work desk was no less orderly, with pens arranged in parallel lines and notepads arranged at perpendicular angles to the pens. He never forgot a deadline, name, or promise, and came to meetings prolifically prepared for any potential outcome. His impressive organizational abilities allowed him to corral together a crew of scrappy interns and hourly workers to build a product with the same integrity of a full-time team, and with a keen awareness of how he spent his time, he artfully arranged his calendar with a balanced blend of work and fun. His life was nothing if not in control, and with an antenna piqued for issues, Nick maintained a state of ease so long as not a hair strayed out of place. As we grew closer, I learned that Nick was a perfectionist in every area of his life but one: much to my dismay, he wasn't conscientious when it came to his diet, and mostly lived off of grilled cheese, pizza, and free fig bars from the office pantry.

It was clear to me how Nick's entrepreneurial success was largely due to his conscientiousness, and so I didn't think of it as anything more than a sweet tick at best or buzzing annoyance at worst. But as time passed and Nick's company began to fumble, his perfectionistic impulses began to control his every thought and action, with no notion left undeliberated and no emotion left unruminated. His mind looped in agonizing circles about things done and undone, and he grew deeply anxious as his company spiraled further out of his control. I watched as he reactively stung everyone who tried to take control of his company's strategy, and rigidly rejected any insinuation that there was a better way of doing things. His once collaborative company became a one-man show as he began to build products and processes in a way that only *he* understood, and with a heartbreaking desperation, he began hoarding responsibilities in fear of losing relevance. For the first time in his life, he stopped showing up to meetings and responding to emails, refusing to indulge anything that threatened the status quo, and not so subtly insisted that people keep their smudgy fingerprints off his immaculate creation.

It was only a matter of months before there was no more company, no more tidy desk, and no more spreadsheets, and I helplessly watched as Nick struggled to navigate this new, discombobulated reality in which everything felt topsy-turvy and hopelessly out of control. Nick had worked so hard to arrange his work and life to his liking, and it was painful to watch his carefully constructed hive smash to the ground. Our relationship grew increasingly turbulent in the wake of his loss, and in an effort to regain control, Nick rerouted his controlling tendencies into other, not so helpful endeavors, like monitoring my social media for new male friends, or rereading my blog posts that talked about past relationships. I cared so much for this sweet bee who flew into my life, and all I wanted was to help him rebuild, reorganize, and find peace, but it was clear that this was a lesson he needed to learn on his own. In a messy end to a sweet relationship, we not so easily parted ways.

But like the bold entrepreneurial spirit he is, Nick decided to heal his relationship with control by throwing every shred of perfectionism, orderliness, and obsessive conscientiousness to the wind. These days, Nick's life is nothing if not unpredictable ... in a good way. In a fit of housecleaning, he sold his apartment, sent his cat to his parents, and decided to travel the world in search of a more sustainable relationship with control. I heard from Nick for the first time in a year when a blue text box popped up on my phone, and of all places, he was messaging me from a cafe in rural South America, perhaps the furthest thing from his orderly life in D.C. I couldn't imagine a better remedy for his consciousness soul, and as is the case with so many entrepreneurs, Nick always learned best by diving into his lessons, fully and unapologetically. Bit by bit, he's rebuilding his hive with more honey and less sting, learning to trust the direction of the winds with every gust. And in the meantime, I simply pray he's left his spreadsheets at home.

The Light

According to Greek mythology, chaos was the first thing to exist, and out of chaos came order ... and perhaps this was the point that the heavens created the entrepreneurial spirit. The Orderly Creator is born with a destiny belief—a divine responsibility of sorts—to create order and control, feeling as though the world then might fall into a state of disorder without their capable efforts. This noble calling is what compels the Orderly Creator to not only create structure in their own lives, but also to create products and services that bring the vast amounts of chaos in the universe into blissful, tidy harmony. There's nothing more soothing to the Orderly Creator than the perfect line of code, properly functioning software integration, or the neatly organized expense report, as these are tiny but important indications that they are successfully in control of their otherwise unwieldy work. Bestowed with an uncanny privilege that few ever truly embrace, the Orderly Creator not only creates the *stuff* that fills the world, but they create their own destinies. Those around the Orderly Creator may poke fun at their fussy rituals and particular ways of navigating life, but these tendencies are born from the same wiring that ensures airtight products and timely paychecks. While it's now a popular metaphysical mantra that we "create our own reality," it's as if the Orderly Creator knew this all along: the best way to predict one's future is, indeed, to create it.

While conscientiousness—the tendency to be orderly, reliable, principled, and self-controlled[114]—is an all but required resource in the entrepreneurial ecosystem, the Orderly Creator can at times be an enigma. As children, they may have been *anything* but diligent when it came to schoolwork or chores, but were steadfastly dutiful in their after-school work or activity of choice. In a funny way, conscientiousness rarely seems to touch *every* aspect of the Orderly Creator's lives, and they often have many tendencies that are anything but organized and thoughtful. But when they decide to impart control over something, they tend to do so with fervor and ferocity, creating structure as if the fates depended on it. For instance, the Orderly Creator may keep a messy home but an impeccable inbox, or may be a reckless adventurer, but cautious fundraiser. Indeed, while their investor report may be an carefully crafted declaration, they may be surprisingly disheveled in their pursuit of play and fun, and the Orderly Creator is often just as organized as they are eager to blow off steam. Whether it's their fussy diet, methodical organization of meetings, or prolific use of spreadsheets, the Orderly Creator's conscientiousness always finds a way of shining through, often despite abundant evidence to the contrary.

While some individuals view traditional employment as an in-convenience, the Orderly Creator often reports it as an unrighteous indignity to have little control over their professional destiny. They have strong opinions about how employees should be managed, systems should be built, or office furniture should be laid out, and yearn to control their schedule, environment, and work product. Maddened by their inability to establish structure the way they see fit, the Orderly Creator often grows stifled by the methods and routines of the powers that be, wanting to impart control over a business that is, frustratingly, not their own. Upon their departure from traditional employment, the Orderly Creator is often overjoyed and overwhelmed to learn that entrepreneurship allows for no finger pointing, no fallback options, and no dilution of responsibility. They quickly realize that conscientiousness isn't a

---

[114] Thompson, E. R. (2008). Development and validation of an international English big-five mini-markers. *Personality and individual differences*, 45(6), 542-548.

nicety, but a true entrepreneurial imperative, and it's not a career in which victims thrive. While this can be an intimidating prospect, the Orderly Creator who is up for the challenge will find entrepreneurship a most satisfying career: it's a path that demands full accountability over one's life, and those who can trustfully channel their conscientious tendencies into their work can truly create their own version of reality.

Conscientiousness is tied to both the intention to become an entrepreneur as well as entrepreneur performance,[115] and there's a *negative* relationship between conscientiousness and work avoidance.[116] The Orderly Creator relishes goals, structure, deadlines, and accountability, and has an astounding ability to control their impulses and delay gratification[117]—at least in *some* domains. The ability to set rules and procedures facilitates the transformation of the Orderly Creator's impractical dreams into tangible reality, as without the discipline and restraint of conscientiousness, it would be nearly impossible to translate their visionary, optimistic minds into practical, operational outcomes. Indeed, conscientiousness weaves threads of caution and restraint into an otherwise eager personality, and the Orderly Creator ensures that even the most audacious decisions are made with care, applying much-needed diligence to an oft-erratic operation. With a low tolerance for disorder, the Orderly Creator is often unintentionally comedic in their tendencies, navigating the world with whiteboards, to-do lists, buzzing notifications, and outsourced schedulers organizing the details of their work, but despite these sweetly neurotic tendencies, when the conscientious personality is supplemented by an openness to experience and a hint of disagreeability, success is all but guaranteed.[118]

---

[115] Zhao, H., Seibert, S. E., & Lumpkin, G. T. (2010). The relationship of person-ality to entrepreneurial intentions and performance: A meta-analytic review. *Journal of Management*, 36, 381-404.

[116] Bipp, T., Steinmayr, R., & Spinath, B. (2008). Personality and achievement motivation: Relationship among Big Five domain and facet scales, achievement goals, and intelligence. *Personality and Individual Differences*, 44, 1454-1464.

[117] Brandstätter, H. (2011). Personality aspects of entrepreneurship: A look at five meta-analyses. *Personality and individual differences*, 51(3), 222-230.

The Dark

The Orderly Creator is often dismayed to realize that entrepreneurship offers a cruel kind of control: while it offers unparalleled freedom, this freedom is matched by unpredictability. Entrepreneurship is arguably the most uncontrollable career one can choose, and while the Orderly Creator can control certain aspects of their environment, such as when, how, and with whom they work, the outcome of their efforts is largely out of control. In the game of new venture creation, effort does not always equate to success, nor do controlling behaviors result in actual control. To cope with this clunky lack of control, the Orderly Creator may come to rely too heavily on their fussy tendencies, finding the slope between constructive conscientiousness and controlling perfectionism mighty slippery as they attempt to organize what is fundamentally chaotic. The Orderly Creator may experience great distress if they begin to lose control of their tightly held preferences or idealized destiny, unable to loosen the grip of their perfectionistic impulses. Whether the loss of control is acute, like a disorganized meeting, or chronic, like a struggling business, the Orderly Creator may find themselves fighting in vain against the rickety unpredictability of entrepreneurship.

The Orderly Creator may be prone to perfectionism and anxiety,[119] and struggle with compulsive tendencies that prevent them from acting swiftly and decisively.[120] Known for fussing with calendars, obsessing over misaligned website features, or micromanaging employees, the Orderly Creator may have an extreme attention to detail which they channel into tasks or activities that give them a false sense of control.[121] Anecdotally, it seems as though they are

---

[118] Gladwell, M (2014). Presentation at World Economic Business Forum in New York.

[119] Carter, N. T., Guan, L., Maples, J. L., Williamson, R. L., & Miller, J. D. (2016). The downsides of extreme conscientiousness for psychological well being: The role of obsessive compulsive tendencies. *Journal of personality*, *84*(4), 510-522.

[120] Ostendorf, F. (2000). Personality disorders and the Five-Factor Model of Personality. A Meta-analysis. Paper presented at the Symposium on personality disorders and five personality factors in Europe and Use. O.P. John (Chair) in the 4th European conference on personality disorders, June 21-24, Paris, France.

particularly likely to resist changes that are enforced from without, and may try to maintain positions of control through misguided corrective action, like sweeping power grabs or complete product overhauls. With a hypervigilance to errors and mistakes, the Orderly Creator may struggle to trust others with their work, and exert perfectionistic control over their employees and co-founders. In romantic relationships, it seems the Orderly Creator often expects partners to sync with their rhythms and preferences, finding themselves flustered when partners want to create their *own* version of reality. This isn't to say the Orderly Creator is intentionally domineering, but it can be a challenging realization that someone else's destiny looks very different from their own.

While some of the Orderly Creator's self-regulatory behaviors are clearly adaptive, like the ability to delay gratification to accomplish a work task, there are maladaptive consequences of *too* much self-control.[122] Self-control both consumes *and* demands internal resources, and the Orderly Creator may find themselves depleted if they cannot replenish their internal stores. It seems these particular souls struggle to do anything half-heartedly, instead adopting the most extreme version of any activity, and this is often seen in the Orderly Creator who adopts extreme health regimens, rigid sleep or eating habits, and inflexible preferences: they don't just exercise, they exercise for three hours a day. They don't just eat healthy, they cut out half of the food pyramid. They don't just dress well, they must have everything perfectly pressed. It's both comical and disheartening how popular such extreme regimens have become among entrepreneurs, and this seems to reflect a need to maintain false yet comforting feelings of control. Indeed, there are very real costs to these incessant self-regulatory behaviors, and it's believed that exerting extreme self-control in one sphere of one's life leads to impaired capacity to regulate in another,[122] which for example may explain why the Orderly Creator with a controlled work regimen may have an uncontrolled relationship with alcohol.

---

[121] Kaiser, R. B., LeBreton, J. M., & Hogan, J. (2015). The dark side of personality and extreme leader behavior. *Applied Psychology*, 64(1), 55-92.

[122] Baumeister, R. F., & Alquist, J. L. (2009). Is there a downside to good self-control?. *Self and Identity*, 8(2-3), 115-130.

To Integrate

The Orderly Creator who errs on the side of extreme conscientiousness tends to be guilty of only one thing: they wish to harmonize a chaotic reality. With controlling tendencies that are born from a place of love, it can be particularly challenging for the Orderly Creator to accept what is and isn't theirs to nudge into place. There is often a point on the Orderly Creator's journey when they recognize the limitations of their ability to control destiny, and this tends to manifest as a moment of both crisis *and* potential growth. While this crisis, often in the form of failure, may seem catastrophic in the moment, it's a critical inflection point during which the Orderly Creator will be forced to either let go and trust, or continue to experience overwhelming conflict and tension. But these painful moments can also teach the Orderly Creator to accept the fates, trust themselves, and embody the lesson that some things shouldn't be fussed with, some outcomes can't be predicted, and some people refuse to be managed. To learn this lesson, the Orderly Creator must understand what is rightfully theirs to fix... and surrender the rest.

The Orderly Creator can integrate their light and dark by developing a greater capacity for *trust* in themselves and others. Trust implies a willingness to release what's not meant to be controlled and embrace any outcome, and while the Orderly Creator often pushes back at this idea, equating it with passivity and submission, trust is nonetheless at the heart of resilience. The Orderly Creator can never be truly resilient if they're always fighting against reality, and it's only through trust that their nervous system can relax into the consistently capricious nature of creation. One of the most common questions the Orderly Creator asks is, *How do I stop worrying about what's out of my control?* and this is the true and unpopular answer: do the work and trust the outcome. When the Orderly Creator puts in the effort to secure the outcome they want, they must let themselves sink into a sense of trust, willing to wake up tomorrow and engage with whatever outcome arises. Only when the Orderly Creator is receptive to the inherent unpredictability of creation can they truly create with sturdiness and sustainability, for there will always be one more thing to control. After the work is done, all the Orderly Creator can do is gracefully trust their hero's journey, palms face up.

- Practice meditation and breathing exercises to "let go" and release control.
- Develop a relationship outside of work characterized by trust (pet, romantic relationship, etc.).
- Consider your faith and destiny (religious, spiritual, philosophical, scientific, etc.).
- Spend time visualizing the outcome you want without attachment to the process.
- Cultivate a workplace culture of trust, vulnerability, and tolerance for failure.
- Spend time in poses and stretches of surrender, like pigeon or happy baby pose.
- Create a mantra around trust (e.g., "I have done my best and trust the outcome").
- Incorporate more spontaneity into your life and work (improv, creative hobbies, etc.).
- Reframe mistakes and challenges as opportunities for growth.
- Use the lessons of nature to guide your trust beliefs (death/renewal, seasonality, symbiosis).

Prompts for Deeper Self-Study

- Do you need structure and order in everything you do? If so, consider how you might find more peace amidst chaos.
- Do you feel anxious when you can't control your environment? If so, consider how you might cultivate a greater capacity for surrender.
- Do you often micromanage others? If so, consider how you might develop more trusting relationships.

- Do you often find yourself lost in the details of your work? If so, consider how you might zoom out to see the big picture.
- Do you feel hyperattentive to issues in your environment? If so, consider how you might learn to accept and embrace flaws and mishaps.

Chapter 11:
The Charming Creator

The Charming Creator		
Dimension: Charisma	**Light Qualities**	**Dark Qualities**
• Ability to attract, charm, influence, and evoke liking • Promotion of self and company as highly competent • Comradery with others • Use of smiling, flattery, and favors • Ability to sway others' beliefs • Tendency to project images of integrity	Convincing; persuasive; influential; accommodating; poised; magnetic; compelling; impressive; sociable	Manipulative; fake; insincere; disingenuous; conforming; suppressed; inauthentic; sneaky; deceitful; shrewd
Motivation: To woo and impress **Mantra:** Fake it till you make it **Tension:** Seduction vs. deception	**To Integrate** Authenticity	

A Fabulous Fox

I never knew which Lana I was going to sit across from each night.

Watching Lana work a room was like watching an impeccably choreographed dance—she navigated any crowd with the sly ease of a fox, and knew how to change the tone of her voice, arc of her spine, and glint in her eye to match whatever the situation demanded. The founder of a well-known company in town, Lana swayed and swashbuckled her way through the city's social circles, and had an uncanny ability to slip seamlessly into any environment without appearing the slightest bit out of place. Whether it was a hoodie-adorned pitch meeting, a hippy-dippy music festival, or five-course dinner at the fanciest restaurant in D.C., Lana had a funny way of fitting in everywhere and nowhere. I swear she even *looked* different across her various lives, transforming her entire mystique from a buttoned-up professional to flirtatious vixen to doting friend at a moment's notice. She always seemed to be perfectly *fine*, and with charm, poise, and disarming ease, convinced you that she had everything under control. Though I never felt she was dishonest and I truthfully admired the flexibility of her mind and spirit, there was always a part of me that wanted to know who the *real* Lana was.

I was introduced to Lana through a mutual friend, and was pleasantly surprised to learn that she had just moved into my neighborhood. I was immediately taken by Lana's uncanny social intelligence, and starting on our first friend-date, she quickly learned to manage the slant of my preferences and my playfully serious persona, expertly feeling her way into the cleverest conversation points and offering confidently cool advice. With the polished conversational skills of a politician, Lana gracefully skirted around every sticking point or sensitive subject, and dodged every faux pas or awkward pause. She possessed a gregarious yet reflective spirit and a charm of which she was well aware, and there was nothing we couldn't do together: we went to dive bars as often as hotel bars, and attended rowdy concerts as often as foundation events, and somehow, Lana knew how to be at ease everywhere we went. Between her whip-smart mind and clever tongue, Lana was always prepared with a joke for her friends as well as a thoughtful conversation topic for a refined audience, and I was constantly amazed that she was loved by everyone and yet not completely understood by anyone.

When it came to work, Lana's ability to woo, impress, and cleverly rearrange herself for the person or situation she was in made her a truly terrific saleswoman. She leveraged her ability to sell herself into an ability to sell her company, and artfully translated her social adeptness into measurable business outcomes. With an unparalleled poise, she was able to hire talent that could have worked at the most elite companies, secure advisers who would be a blushing addition to any company's pitch deck, and speak on stages that were objectively out of her pay grade. Wielding a self-concept as flexible as her mind, Lana could pretend to be anyone for anybody and could cleverly amend her identity for the whims of her audience, making impeccably timed shifts to her words and actions to align herself with the stakeholders of the moment. It was as if she walked around with a spotlight that was hard to look away from, and like a seasoned performer, Lana held her power on any stage with a captivating confidence that made her appear to be both an esteemed leader and a relatable entrepreneur next door. There was no questioning it—Lana was a truly fabulous fox.

Perhaps the most impressive part of Lana's performance as a founder and friend was her skilled hold on her emotions. When things were stressful at work, Lana managed to maintain a calm and cool façade, which she felt was all but necessary within a struggling startup. Her apparent emotional sturdiness gave hope to her employees and stakeholders who so desperately clung to faith in the company, and looked to justify their not-insignificant emotional, professional, and financial investments. Although I often worried about the pressures she internalized, I nonetheless respected her willingness to carry the company's burden on her own shoulders, absorbing the shocks so others wouldn't have to. But interestingly, when the situation and its participants *called* for an emotional display—when it would please others for Lana to emote—she was the first to accept the challenge, spinning into fits of joy or frustration or rambunctiousness to arouse cheers from the group. In a strange and convincing way, her emotions seemed to be at the beck and call of the collective, and anyone who knew Lana would tell you—she sure knew how to please a crowd.

But the performance grew uncomfortable to watch as her company took its final breaths. In response to the overwhelming emotional and financial woes of her company, she shapeshifted more and more into what her company needed: a strong and confident founder who knew how to save it and always appeared "fine." But as Lana continued to hide her thoughts and feelings for the benefit of her company, she grew further away from an authentic experience of her emotions, and found herself constantly managing her impression for the person in the room who needed her attention. In the process, Lana lost track of how she felt, what she believed, and who she wanted to be as a founder. Every overwhelming emotion of fear, guilt, shame, and remorse was silenced and smothered within her, and she carried the energetic weight of her feelings like a proud, stoic statue that continued to go onstage, night after night, as if nothing were wrong. But finally, the years of suppressed emotions began to crack through the surface, and when Lana broke, she broke wide open, exposing a decade of unprocessed physical, mental, emotional, and spiritual wounds. Her mind, body, and spirit fell gut-wrenchingly ill, and this time, there was no covering it up.

Perhaps the only thing more shameful to Lana than falling apart was falling apart in front of an audience, and she began to withdraw from our friendship. I empathized so deeply with all of the multitudes that ricocheted off every corner of her being, and I felt energy pulse off of her that was palpably erratic—suppression and release, dissociation and reassociation, denial and admittance. Eventually, she withdrew completely and spent a year in her home with the curtains drawn, pacing the apartment like a fox in a trap. But these days, after a long hibernation, Lana is finding her way out of her foxhole and back into the light. Though the failure of her beloved company was a crushing experience, I know Lana will forever be more thoughtful about hiding too much of herself again. All the clever gazes, feigned smiles, and hollow nods brought her further away from her true self, and ironically, it took an incredible loss to make Lana more anchored in her authentic nature; she had to first distance herself from her true self to realign with the founder she really wanted to be. And take it from someone who had the pleasure of knowing her—it's a self worthy of showing off.

The Light

Many creators encounter a rather curious nuance when first embarking on their endeavors. They assume it's the originality of an idea or the integrity of the operations that will set them on a path of success—if they only work hard enough, then the customers, press attention, and funding will inevitably follow. But this isn't always the case. Creators are often shocked to realize that, when starting a venture, those who are best at presenting *themselves* tend to more rapidly find success.[123] The Charming Creator has a natural ability to woo and win over others by appearing competent and resilient, and more often than not, this allows them to win the hands and purse strings of those who can escort them to success. Across all stages of a company's development, stakeholders tend to invest in the *individual*, not just the idea, and it's not uncommon for money and attention to be showered upon the Charming Creator before an idea even exists. It's human nature to align with those we like, trust, or at the very least, find impressive, and one could argue that those who excel at new venture creation are those with a flair for pageantry. Enter stage right, the Charming Creator.

In ancient times, charisma—Greek for *gift, divine favor,* or *supernatural power*—was said to be a gift from the gods bestowed upon prophets and leaders to help them in their daily tasks,[124] and was believed to be a gift "of the body and spirit not accessible to everybody."[125] Charisma's consequences are only evident in the perceptions of a leader's followers, and the art of charismatic leadership is a deeply social practice in which the Charming Creator not only sells their product, but *themselves*. To accomplish this, the Charming Creator employs an effective leadership tool—impression management—which is the ability to manage one's impression by using techniques (idea conformity, flattery, engaged body language, and the like) that induce positive reactions from others.[126] Impression management

---

[123] Nagy, B. G., Pollack, J. M., Rutherford, M. W., & Lohrke, F. T. (2012). The influence of entrepreneurs' credentials and impression management behaviors on perceptions of new venture legitimacy. *Entrepreneurship Theory and Practice*, 36(5), 941-965.

[124] Conger, J. (2015). Charismatic leadership. *Wiley encyclopedia of management*, 1-2.

[125] Neuwirth, G., Weber, M., & Eisenstadt, S. N. (1969). Max Weber on Charisma and Institution Building. Selected Papers. *Social Forces*, 48(1), 118.

[126] Baron, R. A., & Markman, G. D. (2000). Beyond social capital: How social skills can enhance entrepreneurs' success. *Academy of Management Perspectives*, 14(1), 106-116.

is one of the most common and least discussed phenomena among entrepreneurs, perhaps because the best impression managers don't appear to be "managing" anything. Unlike other careers in which an employee *does* their work, entrepreneurs often feel they *are* their work, and this creates an urgent need to present themselves in a favorable light. The Charming Creator uses impression management to influence the perception of themselves, their ideas, and their creations,[127] and can charismatically navigate even the most nuanced social exchanges to move closer to their goals.

Charismatic leadership has strong effects on leader outcomes, and while charisma can be learned to an extent,[128] it appears to be a largely heritable trait.[129] Whether by nature or nurture, the Charming Creator can be witnessed early on in life as the convincing child who wins the favor and affection of every adult in the room, and the intriguing young adult who boasts many social and romantic relationships. As the Charming Creator begins to explore jobs, they often find themselves in sales, business development, marketing, or other social roles in which their success is largely measured by how well others respond to them. As they move through their career, the Charming Creator is tasked with using their persuasion, salesmanship, and leadership abilities to further a company's agenda, though they often grow depleted by the idea of leveraging their own charisma for the sake of another's bottom line. This frustration prompts the Charming Creator to seek out a career in which they can reap the rewards of their own social energy, and they naturally find entrepreneurship an ideal outlet to translate their ability to sell themselves into an evergreen source of opportunities. Because an entrepreneur's integrity is often equated to the integrity of their company, the Charming Creator who can

---

[127] Singh, R. K., & Krishnan, V. R. (2002). Impact of impression management and value congruence on attributed charisma. NMMS *Management Review, 14*(1), 86-94.

[128] Antonakis, J., Fenley, M., & Liechti, S. (2011). Can charisma be taught? Tests of two interventions. *Academy of Management Learning & Education, 10*(3), 374-396.

[129] Johnson, A. M., Vernon, P. A., McCarthy, J. M., Molson, M., Harris, J. A., & Jang, K. L. (1998). Nature vs nurture: Are leaders born or made? A behavior genetic investigation of leadership style. *Twin Research and Human Genetics, 1*(4), 216-223.

sell themselves will inevitably succeed in selling an extension of themselves: their creation.

While the Charming Creator's flair for impression management may sound inauthentic or disingenuous, this isn't necessarily the case. In its ideal practice, impression management is tactical, not deceptive.[127] The Charming Creator's astounding social and emotional intelligence offers them a true competitive advantage that helps them navigate the complex interpersonal world of entrepreneurship, and they are often able to acutely sense the needs, desires, and preferences of those around them.[127] They can socialize and empathize easily, instinctively placing themselves in the shoes of others, and tasks like sales and networking come entirely naturally to the Charming Creator. Even if they don't *like* sales, they're nonetheless blessed with the ability to sell a product by selling themselves, and leadership positions are not so much a goal as an inevitability for the Charming Creator. Well-practiced in the art of fake it till you make it, the Charming Creator is gifted with a quickness of mind that allows them to assess situational demands rapidly, consider a range of socially appropriate responses, mask "inappropriate" responses, and make quick, humorous come-backs.[130] It also seems, anecdotally speaking, that the Charming Creator exudes strong sexual energy—what the Greeks called *eros*—which, when wielded mindfully, can be a powerful tool to draw the collective into one's court.

The Dark

But the Charming Creator's disingenuous presentation of themselves and their product can be one of the greatest threats to their authenticity, especially if they grow so skilled at impression management that they can't distinguish between performance and reality. The entrepreneurial ecosystem has stigmatized the

---

[130] von Hippel, W., Ronay, R., Baker, E., Kjelsaas, K., & Murphy, S. C. (2016). Quick thinkers are smooth talkers: Mental speed facilitates charisma. *Psychological science, 27*(1), 119-122.

expression of fear, failure, and personal challenges, and Stoicism—
a practice in which adherents are expected to endure pain or
hardship without showing feelings[131]—has been adopted as the
"religion" of entrepreneurs. The Charming Creator often feels
compelled to adhere to these principles of emotional stability and
sturdiness amidst challenge, and this pressure can make them feel
as though they must hide their true self from those with the ability
to determine their future, like investors, customers, and the press.[132]
The Charming Creator who manages their social persona to appear
stoic and in control of their emotions may look like the epitome of
resilience, but the truth is often far from it. Resilience is the ability
to *feel* challenging emotions and *cope* with them, whereas the
suppression of emotions is the *avoidance* or *denial* of negative states,
a process that never allows the Charming Creator to productively
cope with difficult feelings. While Stoicism *can* be practiced
mindfully, it seems to more often act as justification to suppress
and deny challenging emotions.

The Charming Creator often lives in fear that others will eventually
realize everything is not, in fact, *fine*, and out of necessity, creates a
stunning façade to mask the reality of their inner world. While the
Charming Creator's artfully managed persona is often born from
their noble desire to present a strong front for their stakeholders,
it can quickly desensitize them to the reality of their thoughts,
feelings, and embodied reactions. The Charming Creator who
manages their impression to an extreme often dissociates from the
pleas of their body, mind, and spirit for the sake of creation, and
may continue to work despite incredible stresses, fatigue, and
depleting emotions. Indeed, the Charming Creator may become
such a convincing impression manager that they even fool
themselves, not realizing how deeply they're struggling until their
body begins to beg for their attention; the cumulative weight of

---

[131] STOICISM: definition in the Cambridge English Dictionary. (n.d.). Retrieved
from https://dictionary.cambridge.org/us/dictionary/english/stoicism.
[132] Shepherd, D. A., & Haynie, J. M. (2011). Venture failure, stigma, and impression management: A self verification, self-determination view. *Strategic Entrepreneurship Journal*, 5(2), 178-197.

years of suppressed emotions is the source of a great deal of stress-related illness.[133] What is not externalized is often destructively internalized, and when the Charming Creator navigates their work with an insistence on appeasing the collective, they are not only isolated from a connection with others, but from an honest connection with themselves.

The Charming Creator's motivation may not be so much around achievement as it is around the *appearance* of achievement, and there's often a startling gulf between their perceived and actual successes. While the Charming Creator may not be intentionally disingenuous, they can easily find themselves conforming with the opinions of important stakeholders to maintain a state of respect and liking, and use their charisma to woo others for less than righteous reasons. This harmful impression management is often seen as the "everything's great!" line at a networking event, the laugh at a board member's off-color joke, the exaggerated accomplishments on a personal site, and the tolerance of a too-close touch of an investor. While these strategies may be productive in the moment, they also dishonor the Charming Creator's own boundaries and beliefs for the sake of a temporary win. In particular, the act of impression management may be difficult for introverted entrepreneurs who feel the need to display themselves as extroverts, exhausting their social energy in the process. After enough time pleasing others, the Charming Creator often finds themselves unanchored in their own being, unsure of what they actually believe and value, and, in the very worst cases, spreading untruths to maintain a state of social respect. Of all the hazards of entrepreneurship, perhaps the most damaging is the suppression of a creator's vital emotions, the very source of their internal guidance.

---

[133] Gross, J. J., & Levenson, R. W. (1993). Emotional suppression: physiology, self-report, and expressive behavior. *Journal of personality and social psychology*, 64(6), 970.

To Integrate

Like it or not, the Charming Creator has a responsibility to use their *whole* self to create—they must use every feeling, thought, sensation, and firmly held conviction to create with impact. While impression management can be an effective tool to persuade and assuage others, the Charming Creator must never use it as a tool to distance themselves from the instincts and emotions that offer invaluable guidance in the creative process. It's important for the Charming Creator to be firmly anchored in their experience—even if it's ever-changing and occasionally ugly—to create from a solid foundation of intentionality, and should never defer to the preferences of those who aren't loyal and compassionate advisers. By honoring the nature of their own experience, with its positive and negative emotions, strong and conflicting opinions, and often unglamorous personal truths, the Charming Creator will find that they naturally gain the trust and respect of others. Contrary to what many believe, honesty is not an impediment to successful impression management, but can instead be a most essential tool.

The Charming Creator can integrate their light and dark by holding *authenticity* as a sacred imperative. Authenticity reflects the willingness to express one's emotions, assert one's beliefs, and stay true to one's values, regardless of external demands or pressures. The Charming Creator often asks: *but how can I be authentic while also appearing resilient?* This is an understandable question, but it's born from a fundamental misconception that vulnerability will be perceived as weakness. More often than not, the Charming Creator who authentically expresses the good *and* bad of their experience will garner respect and admiration for their vulnerability. Indeed, authentic vulnerability can be used as a tool of endearment to build trust and affiliation, as well as a practical tool to gain an informational advantage and solicit support. While the Charming Creator is often rightfully hesitant to advertise their struggles, it's also one of the surest ways to attract much needed personal and professional reinforcement, and identify true allies in the glittery spectacle of creation. Even though it may not always be obvious, the most impressive impression the Charming Creator can make is one that exposes their fullest, most brilliantly nuanced self, scars included.

- Create a company culture that encourages vulnerability and emotional expression.
- Speak up when someone's words or actions don't sit well with you.
- Spend time re-centering yourself after networking or prolonged interactions.
- Notice if others frequently misconstrue your presence for flirtation or attraction.
- Mind your use of flattery, favors, or other social niceties unless they are deserved.
- Anchor yourself in your own emotions, thoughts, beliefs, and values.
- Engage in activities (exercise, writing, etc.) that release emotional energy from your body.
- Find trusted professional and romantic partners who don't judge your "weaknesses."
- Reflect upon the times your authenticity has earned you sincere respect and affiliation.
- Find peers who can reflect your authentic self back to you, again and again.

Prompts for Deeper Self-Study

- Do you adjust your **beliefs** based on the people you're around? If so, consider how you could express your beliefs more authentically.
- Do you adjust your **values** based on the people you're around? If so, consider what your code of values would include.
- Do you adjust your **emotions** based on the people you're around? If so, consider how you might express yourself more vulnerably.

- Do you worry that others would judge you if they knew the "real" you? If so, consider where you learned this belief and why you believe it to be true.
- Do you often experience stress-related and/or psychosomatic illness? If so, consider how this might be related to your unexpressed inner-world.

Recommended reading for the Charming Creator:
Daring Greatly: How the Courage to Be Vulnerable Transforms the Way We Live, Love, Parent, and Lead by Brené Brown

Chapter 12:
The Courageous Creator

The Courageous Creator		
Dimension: Optimism	Light Qualities	Dark Qualities
• Hopefulness and emotional fortitude • Persistent action orientation • Positive explanatory style • Belief in positive or favorable outcomes • Enhanced creative & innovative thinking • Higher risk tolerance or risk preference	Brazen; decisive; daring; hopeful; resilient; positive; cheery; assured; spirited; upbeat; opportunistic; gritty; brave	Reckless; delusional; impulsive; blind; hasty; ignorant; foolhardy; uninhibited; rash; uninformed; immature
Motivation: To look on the bright side **Mantra:** Yes! **Tension:** Resilience vs. ignorance	To Integrate Intentionality	

A Blind Bull

Chris was a blend of boy next door meets daunting daredevil.

The founder of a New York-based startup, Chris was a card-carrying churchgoer who grew up in a traditional town with puritanical values and clung to traditions that involved brown liquor, American flags, and classic rock-and-roll riffs. As the captain of a sailboat and a member of a few old-boy clubs, Chris seemed to be as clean cut and conventional as founders come. But little did I know, this straight-edged demeanor had enough raw guts behind it to make even the sturdiest souls cringe, all pulled together with a boyishly mischievous smile. We first met at his company's annual holiday party, and while I didn't know anything about the financial health of his startup at the time, I was immediately struck by the audacity of the be-tinseled event. The evening boasted an all-night open bar, a decadent buffet, and an unlimited plus-one policy, which was bold for a startup with an employee headcount you could tick off on one hand. As my friend and I made our way through the crowd in search of the evening's host, a tall, dark-haired man with an Old Fashioned in hand swaggered out from the sea of heads. His optimism pulsed off of him with an undeniable force, and I suddenly understood the courage behind the event that was playing Russian roulette with *someone's* bank account.

Brash, bold, and often belligerent, Chris had the courage of a bull who regularly hurled himself toward red flags with a naive yet sturdy trust that he would be safe. Over the coming months, Chris and I developed a fascinating friendship characterized by a playful naughtiness that felt like the schoolyard rush when you first learn you can break the grown-ups' rules. When I was around Chris, the idea of taking risks seemed far less daunting and far more fun, and he made you feel as if every step out of your comfort zone would inevitably be rewarded. Chris drove fast, played hard, said *yes!* to everyone and everything, and, with his heart boldly smeared across his sleeve, I watched as he valiantly chased woman after stunning woman, pulling off every big and small romantic gesture with a suspiciously practiced ease. There seemed to be nothing that reddened his cheeks in both work and life, and he never apologized for being a little *too much* for everyone else. I waved off his occasional arrogance and foolhardy optimism as an occupational hazard, and we spent a season playing together like thick-skinned little children.

It seemed his startup had nine lives, and I met him during one of its many resurrections. Though his company had seen better days, it nonetheless appeared to be on the up and up, and I trustfully listened as he told me about the "game-changing" pivots he was making. Whenever I asked him about his progress, he quipped something like *Great!* or *Coming along!* and I had no reason to doubt his bold, cheerful commentary. As a founder, Chris viewed failure as an impossibility, and refused to hold space for defeat in his consciousness. If he believed one thing, it was that the fates would always be on the side of his company, and, with a straight face, he would tell you it was *destined* to succeed. His stomach was lined with an authentic blend of optimism and risk tolerance that drew the admiration of employees, colleagues, and investors alike, and when Chris said he could do something—however impossible—you couldn't help but believe him. Even though he had faced dark days as a founder that would have left others raising the white flag, Chris refused to surrender and developed a resilient, proud skin in the process. I'm quite certain that when he slept at night, he dreamed of himself as the weathered captain of a ship that charged ahead through crashing waves, defiantly laughing in the face of disaster and doom.

But after a few months, my friendship with Chris began to disintegrate. Out of the blue, he started to turn down activities, and didn't show any—not even feigned—signs of protest when I offered to pick up the tab. We circled around the issue for several weeks, but I wasn't worried, as I easily recognized the signs of a struggling founder, and figured he'd tell me in his own time. One night, in an effort to be more cost-conscious, I proposed an outing I knew he couldn't turn down: a happy hour tacos and tequila special and a free comedy show. At the very least, he could get two tacos for five bucks and some bargain basement laughs. I was quite certain this itinerary wouldn't be an issue, but low and behold, it *was* an issue, and he took this opportunity to break the news: he had stopped taking a salary several months ago, and started to invest his life savings into the company. His employees had also stopped taking a salary, and were contributing to the company's donation dish. As far as remaining supplies went, he had just about reached the bottom of the barrel, and the company bank account was circling the drain. But strangely, he wasn't as ruffled as I wanted him to be, and maintained a maddening front of stubborn optimism.

I stood for a moment processing this revelatory information, begging my face to not give away the shock that shot across every corner of my brain. I knew things weren't ideal, but I didn't know they were *taco restriction* not ideal. I had known many founders before Chris and thought I had heard it all, but as he was wont to do, he put them all to shame. While Chris wasn't the only entrepreneur I'd known who'd given up a salary or invested his own money, it was the *audacity* with which he did it that startled me. He invested *most*, not some, of his money. He cut *all*, not some, of his salary. He told me the next iteration of the company was going to be huge, and it was only a matter of months before money started to roll in again. With a frenetic hopefulness, he told me that his upcoming product launch would save his company and his pride, and restore his finances once again. Clearly, there was something I wasn't fully understanding, so I began the investigation: was the company making money? *No.* Did the company have a way of making money in the future? *Not really.* Was he planning to cut his losses and jump ship? *Definitely not.*

But Chris was insistent—he was building his dream company, and there wasn't anything else he'd rather do. If he could give his money away again, he would, and he wasn't planning to stop the bleeding anytime soon. Even though he didn't know where his next meal would come from, he believed that respite was only a few months away, and no matter which way I tried to make my case, there was simply no reasoning with him. He was too optimistic to admit defeat and too stubborn to change course. Like a blind bull, he launched himself into yet another fighting ring, but this time, he wouldn't emerge unscarred. I had grown to adore the trust he had in himself, the universe, or some other divine force that he would be protected, and it was painful to watch him accept that the fates were not always so accommodating. As the weeks passed, the truth about his new reality began to sink in, and I believe it was the first time he recognized failure as a probability. This affronting realization struck him to his core, and, bit by bit, his sprightly optimism transformed into dark dejection. His face hollowed, mojo fizzled, and he began to look like his bank account: spent, tired, and desperate for a fresh infusion.

While it was hard watching him lick his financial and reputational wounds, I was perhaps most disheartened by the idea that he would lose the optimism that defined the essence of his being. I worried that his sweet trust in the world would forever be tarnished. But ever the steadfast spirit, Chris pulled himself together and stubbornly decided to carry on, continuing his business as a one-man operation, just him, his dog, and his slightly diminished appetite for risk. He sent me a message a few months later saying that he still had hope in the future of his company, and was continuing to work steadfastly in the confines of his apartment. Sighing, I told him I didn't know whether his persistence was crazy brave or just plain crazy, and in response, he simply said, "It's the question I haven't yet answered."

The Light

It can be difficult for many to understand the rose-tinted lens through which the Courageous Creator views the world. While others age out of their trusting belief that the world is a hospitable place, the Courageous Creator maintains an enviable, youthful innocence, believing that anything is possible, and the universe is generally benevolent. Others grow up, becoming taller and ever further from the ground, but the Courageous Creator clings to the idea that even the most daunting falls end in only scrapes and bruises. The optimism of the Courageous Creator is often misunderstood if not entirely rejected by the logical, objective thinkers of the world, and it could be argued that much of the resentment toward entrepreneurs is due to this sprightliness of spirit. Pragmatists may scoff at the Courageous Creator's sincere belief in a positive future, but this optimism is all but necessary in the harsh landscape of new venture creation,[134] and is a characteristic of successful leaders who wish to attract an

---

[134] James, N., & Gudmundsson, A. (2011). Entrepreneur optimism and the new venture creation process. *Journal of Asia Entrepreneurship and Sustainability, 7*(2), 52-71.

improbable reality.[135] The hardened corner of so many adult hearts seems to stay soft in the entrepreneurial spirit, and while others struggle to embody the invincibility they once felt as children, the Courageous Creator clings to shreds of this trust and faith.

Entrepreneurs are particularly high in dispositional optimism—the tendency to expect positive outcomes despite the lack of rational justification for those expectations[136]—and the line between hope and naiveté is one the Courageous Creator dances upon often. While skeptical stakeholders may assign an "optimism discount" to the Courageous Creator whose valuation is decorated with tinsel or projections mimic suspiciously steep cliffs, these chirpy spirits nonetheless maintain an enviable advantage compared to their pessimistic counterparts.[137] It's not an unfounded notion that entrepreneurs must have a just-irrational-enough mindset to enter entrepreneurship, as a realistic perspective might be far too damning; if the Courageous Creator were to rationally weigh the odds of success, they would likely never begin. While there's a statistically higher likelihood of venture failure than success, nearly all businesses are started by people who are certain they'll succeed, and it seems the gutsy souls who embark on the entrepreneurial journey rarely entertain the notion that the house will win. Few people trust themselves enough to take the risks required in new venture creation, and the Courageous Creator who can distort their reality *just enough* has sufficient resilience built into their worldview to tolerate the ride. It could be argued that staunch rationality is a prohibitive characteristic of the aspiring entrepreneur, and that dopamine-fueled optimism[138]—allowing for the *selective* avoidance of

[135] Peterson, S.J., Walumbwa, F.O., Byron, K. & Myrowitz, J. (2009). CEO positive psychological traits, transformational leadership, and firm performance in high-technology start-up and established firms. *Journal of Management, 35*, 348-368.

[136] Hmieleski, K. M., & Baron, R. A. (2009). Entrepreneurs' optimism and new venture performance: A social cognitive perspective. *Academy of management Journal, 52*(3), 473-488.

[137] Dushnitsky, G. (2010). Entrepreneurial optimism in the market for technological inventions. *Organization Science, 21*(1), 150-167.

[138] Sharot, T., Riccardi, A. M., Raio, C. M., and Phelps, E. A. (2007). Neural mechanisms mediating optimism bias. *Nature, 450*, 102-105.

reality—can be a true competitive advantage for the entrepreneurial spirit.

The Courageous Creator can be spotted early on in life by the myriad manifestations of their can-do nature: they're the child who argues with a teacher when they're told something is impossible, the bullish teenager with a blooming portfolio of side businesses, and the smirking, brash young adult who believes everything will work out in their favor. Those who come into the world with optimism vibrating through their being may find themselves at odds with an oft-pessimistic world, particularly in school and traditional work environments; the Courageous Creator's hope is often all but crushed in employment settings in which naysayers slow their pace, condemn their enthusiasm, and remind them of what's *not* possible. When the Courageous Creator's nature is to believe that anything is possible, this negativity can feel entirely suffocating, and they often struggle to understand why others are scared to just *do it*. The transition from employment to entrepreneurship often begins when the Courageous Creator leaves—or is asked to leave— their role after they've faced too many denied requests for action, or their employer finds fault with their appetite for risk and opportunism. Telling the Courageous Creator *It won't work*, or *You can't*, or *It's too risky* is more than sufficient kindling to spark an act of enthusiastic defiance, and is the start of many an entrepreneurial journey.

But far from a reckless affliction of today's youth, entrepreneurial optimism may in fact be as old as humankind. It's believed that entrepreneurs are descendants of early humans who faced competition and uncertainty, making bets with their resources and lives, in the hope of creating a more prosperous future.[139] For those optimistic explorers whose appetite for adventure didn't end in death or disability, there was often a great unclaimed reward on the other side, and the Courageous Creator is likely the modern-day

---

[139] Johnson, D. D., & Fowler, J. H. (2011). The evolution of overconfidence. *Nature*, 477(7364), 317.

bearer of our ancestral belief in the viability of the impossible; they are strung with the collective optimism of every venturer who bravely carved out the world we live in today. Indeed, it's quite useful that the mind of the Courageous Creator is rather like the mind of the tipsy—confident, colorful, and a touch cocky—as this optimism, particularly when combined with the hypomanic tendencies of many entrepreneurs,[140] can take the edge off a career fraught with risk and uncertainty. Buttressed by their optimism and unconstrained by the fatalistic mentality that inhibits so many, the Courageous Creator is able to see opportunities everywhere, rarely faces the challenge of having too *few* goals, and can be counted on to say yes to everything.[141] This optimism also spills over into their creative endeavors, and enables the Courageous Creator to take both business and creative risks, think more vividly and expansively about the future, and construct hopeful realities that others wouldn't dare to dream.

The Dark

But when the manic energy of the Courageous Creator mingles with high-risk decisions of new venture creation, they often find themselves charging at red flags, blinded by the same optimism that's served them so well. Excessive optimism is believed to be the primary reason for the high incidence of new venture failure,[142] and is largely credited to poor or irrational decision making[143] and un-checked fantasizing.[144] But while it may seem obvious in hindsight

---

[140] Eckblad, M., & Chapman, L. J. (1986). Development and validation of a scale for hypomanic personality. *Journal of abnormal psychology*, 95(3), 214.

[141] Segerstrom, S. C., & Nes, L. S. (2006). When goals conflict but people prosper: The case of dispositional optimism. *Journal of Research in Personality*, 40(5), 675-693.

[142] Gartner, J. (2005). America's manic entrepreneurs: energy, creativity, and risk-taking propensity have made us the most successful nation in the world. You can partly thank the genes of our most inventive citizens. *The American Enterprise*, 16(5), 18-22.

[143] Palich, L. & Bagby, D. (1995). Using Cognitive Theory to Explain Entrepreneurial Risk Taking: Challenging Conventional Wisdom. *Journal of Business Venturing*, 10, 425 – 438.

[144] Coelho, C., De Meza, D. & Reyniers, D. (2004). Irrational exuberance, entrepreneurial finance and public policy. *International Tax and Public Finance*, 11, 391-417.

that the overinvestment of personal funds or the rapid hiring of employees was rather reckless, such choices can seem all but logical in the moment. These shortsighted misses are born from the same wiring that empowers the Courageous Creator to take admirable risks, and the line between impulsivity and decisiveness can be imperceptibly fine. What seems unfathomable to others is often a necessity in the mind of the Courageous Creator, and such ill-fated decisions are rarely as intentionally reckless as they seem. Many resilient leaders have been victim to their own optimism, and while the media is quick to slap the wrists of those who make reckless bets, they are just as quick to celebrate when those bets pay off. It can be difficult for the Courageous Creator to be shamed and saluted for the same quality, especially when their optimism can make them look like a hero just as often as a fool.

The Courageous Creator finds themselves at odds with their optimism when they completely, not selectively, ignore reality. Between unrealistic expectations, discounting negative advice, and conveniently rearranging information to avoid contradiction,[145] the Courageous Creator can manifest such a delusional version of reality that it's nearly impossible to create intentional strategies and trusting relationships. While the Courageous Creator's optimism may attract to them a range of potentialities, they may find themselves so excited by all of their options that they experience crushing goal conflict, lost in a maelstrom of overextension and indecision.[146] Beyond the damage they can inflict upon their own success and well-being, the Courageous Creator is also eager to spread their optimistic beliefs to others, often in a rather reckless fashion. While they have only the most generous intentions, the Courageous Creator may encourage others to make jumps for which they are professionally or emotionally unprepared, and it can

---

[145] Geers, A. L., & Lassiter, G. D. 2002. Effects of affective expectations on affective experience: The moderating role of optimism-pessimism. *Personality and Social Psychological Bulletin*, 28: 1026-1039.
[146] Segerstrom, S. C., & Nes, L. S. (2006). When goals conflict but people prosper: The case of dispositional optimism. *Journal of Research in Personality*, 40(5), 675-693.

be all too easy for them to offer the overly enthusiastic advice of *Just do it!*. This sunny mentorship is the unfortunate source of many misguided ventures, and while today's creators are not as likely to experience the *fatal* outcomes of our optimistic ancestors, they may nonetheless harm themselves, their companies, and their reputations in the process.

It's often terribly frustrating to those around the Courageous Creator to listen to their fearless declarations of the impossible, finding themselves voiceless as they try to protect their loved one or colleague from the damage they can inflict upon themselves. But, in defense of the Courageous Creator's optimism, this buoyancy may be a dynamic adaption process that helps them overlook too-harsh truths and unfavorable odds.[147] Indeed, if the Courageous Creator were to ruminate on the depths of their professional, reputational, and financial risk, they would likely be so racked with worry that they'd render themselves impotent. While the *selective* avoidance of reality can be psychologically useful, the Courageous Creator who is unable or unwilling to see how their optimism is harmful may find themselves removing guardrails, often in the form of people and processes meant to protect them.[146] They may avoid people who try to shield them from harm, writing them off as naysayers, or disregard evidence that contradicts their hopeful dreams. But for the Courageous Creator who learns best by experience, they must often bear a great loss to understand the limitations of optimism, as a treacherous fall is a mighty effective way to learn about the unforgiving tug of gravity.

To Integrate

Optimism is perhaps the most contagious energy one can experience in a roomful of entrepreneurial spirits, and is arguably their most admired trait: without their belief in the viability of the

---

[147] Ayala, J. C., & Manzano, G. (2014). The resilience of the entrepreneur. Influence on the success of the business. A longitudinal analysis. *Journal of Economic Psychology*, *42*, 126-135.

impossible, our progress as a society would move far slower, and would certainly be less exciting. There's something unspeakably motivating about a career in which *anything* is possible, and everyone around you believes that to be true. It's most essential that the Courageous Creator never lose their trusting, child's mind, but it's also important that they learn to keep at least *one* foot firmly rooted in reality. Soaring on the wings of optimism, it's easy to fly too close to the sun, and it's often through a tumble that the Courageous Creator learns about the inevitable fallibility of creation. While painful, this moment of being burned and awakening to the limits of optimism can teach the Courageous Creator a most crucial lesson: how to keep one eye gazing upward and the other staring at a steady totem on the ground.

The Courageous Creator can integrate their light and dark by increasing their capacity for *intentionality* in their personal and business dealings. To create with intention requires the Courageous Creator to act with deliberate purpose, mindful awareness, and a willingness to see things as they truly are. Intention invites the Courageous Creator to slow down, pay attention, and recognize the value of plans, foresight, and structure, especially if it may save them from the edge of self-induced deception. When surrounded by colleagues who allow for too much delusion, risk, impulse, and recklessness, the Courageous Creator must temper their speed, and muster the counter-intuitive courage to insist upon safeties. To pad their optimism, the Courageous Creator might prioritize intentional co-founders, processes to inform decision making, and techniques that shepherd their thoughts and actions into a place of heightened awareness. It would be the greatest shame if the Courageous Creator were to see reality *so* clearly that they were discouraged from chasing their grandest dreams, but there's no need to relearn the harsh lessons faced by so many venturers before them.

- Make a habit of asking for advice and being mindful when offering advice to others.

- Spend time grounding your energy in a quiet, steady environment.
- Find a cofounder or partner who's more practical and detail-oriented than you.
- Allow yourself a reflection period before making big decisions.
- Use meditation as a tool to slow down your thoughts, actions, and emotions.
- Avoid making decisions if your energy feels particularly "manic" (intensely energized, euphoric, etc.).
- Keep an open-ear when others express doubt, concern, or caution around a decision.
- Reflect upon the opportunities you've pursued and when optimism has/hasn't served you.
- Recognize cycles of reckless/impulsive behavior and ask those around you to identify them.
- Make it more difficult to act impulsively by establishing checks and balances.

Prompts for Deeper Self-Study

- Do you make quick, impulse decisions? If so, consider how your decisions could be more intentional.
- Do you avoid people or processes that discourage your optimism? If so, consider how these people or processes might benefit you.
- Do you avoid thinking about negative outcomes? If so, consider how you might incorporate a more realistic lens in your decision making.
- Do you seek out and enjoy risk, personally and professionally? If so, consider the ways you can enjoy the thrill of risk without its depleting consequences.
- Do you feel compelled to say *yes* to every person and opportunity? If so, consider how you might prioritize your energetic investments.

Recommended reading for the Courageous Creator:
The Hypomanic Edge: The Link Between (A Little) Craziness and (A Lot Of) Success in America by John D. Gartner Ph.D.

Chapter 13:
The Existential Creator

The Existential Creator		
Dimension: Self-Actualization	Light Qualities	Dark Qualities
• Expansion of personal boundaries • Realization of creative, intellectual & social potential • Experience of emotions like gratitude and awe • Belief in spiritual or greater sense of connectedness • Self-expression that is authentic and vulnerable • Feelings of meaning, fulfillment and wholeness • Tendency to be lost and absorbed by experience	Wise; serious; contemplative; soulful; fulfilled; intentional; reflective; grateful; mystical; philosophical; purposeful; impactful	Disillusioned; depressive; bitter; ruminative; hopeless; broody; heavy; unfulfilled; melancholy; pensive; dejected; discouraged; lost; haunted
Motivation: To find meaning **Mantra:** Live your purpose **Tension:** Realization vs. disillusion	**To Integrate** Joy	

A Heavy Elephant

Perhaps the best way to describe Michael would be *broody*.

With wry humor and perpetually crossed arms, Michael exuded a seriousness that I found darkly, tragically intriguing. The founder of a local tech startup who was unconditionally devoted to his company, Michael smirked more than he smiled, gazed more than he glanced, and was prone to bouts of wallowing gloominess that somehow fit him perfectly. With the sulky confidence of a romance novel character, he was broodingly handsome, unironically poetic, and wrenchingly self-reflective, and these qualities made for a persona that was understood by few and resented by many, especially when compared to the chirping, quipping enthusiasm of many of his colleagues. We both had offices in the same coworking space, and though his tempestuous charm caught my eye, I didn't know what to make of him first. His lips were always pouty and brows were always furrowed, and I rather quickly decided I disliked his dramatic disposition. I found his temperamental nature to be childlike and couldn't understand why such a captivating fellow would choose to be so *intense*. But nonetheless, there was something about his melancholic energy that drew my attention, and I couldn't help but track his swaggering steps every time he sullenly paced to and from the coffee dispenser.

We crossed paths in the coworking kitchen for several weeks until, one night, our connection became all but inevitable. I was out at a bar with coworkers when I spotted him standing in a corner with a whisky in hand, intensely gazing at the crowd under fittingly dim, atmospheric lighting. Emboldened by a second cocktail and just enough brushed-shoulder encounters, I made my way across the room, and with a disarming ease, we clicked into place like two old, familiar souls. In the middle of that noisy, drunken bar, I started one of the most intense relationships I had ever been in, characterized by all the feverishness one would expect from such a mercurial spirit. Like two nocturnal creatures, we were both pleasantly surprised to find someone else who also liked to muse about the darker side of the day, and we resonated with the unflattering burdens we thought we carried alone. We stood witness to each other's murkiness and embraced it, and navigated a deep, dark, and nothing if not dramatic moonlit romance. He was the last person I thought I'd be with but exactly the one I needed, and he taught me how to appreciate his surprisingly common breed of spiritualist entrepreneur.

After knowing him for a short time, it became clear why Michael was drawn to entrepreneurship: he possessed an unflinching desire to self-actualize through his work, and chose the path of a founder as a means to do so. The challenges of entrepreneurship made him confront his light and dark, forcing him to reconcile the two, and like so many entrepreneurs, Michael used his heaviness as a source of creative inspiration and existential motivation. He launched a technology business inspired by a vision of how the world *could* be—once he saw the solution in his mind's eye, it couldn't be unseen. Almost as if the vision chose him and he was a mere vehicle for its creation, once his calling took hold of him, he had no choice but to devote his energy into seeing it through. To start his company, he dropped out of an elite business school, worked for months at poverty level, and survived off free snacks from the coworking pantry. While his work wasn't always easy, he savored the blissful confluence of his spirit and his mission, and viewed his company as a vessel to do good in the world. It was a means to channel his energy into something bigger than himself, and it filled him with a sense of purpose that his soul so desperately craved. For the first time, the void between him and his potential was growing smaller, and he was beginning to catch glimpses of a truly meaningful life.

Far from the melodramatic moodiness that others saw in him, I began to see how his melancholy nature was the driver of his entrepreneurial ambition—he regularly plumbed his own depths for a more profound understanding of his intention, and, as if for fun, turned himself inside out to maintain alignment with his life's purpose. He cared surprisingly little about the money or fame that entrepreneurship could offer him, and though he often frustrated me with his piousness, I admired the value he placed on the intrinsic worthiness of work. Unlike colleagues who fretted about wearing the latest trends or posting their most recent success story, Michael's anxieties were mostly existential in nature, and he instead ran toward personal and professional challenges that made him *just* uncomfortable enough to grow. I sometimes wondered why he seemed to invite crisis into his life quite on purpose, but I soon realized that he collided with obstacles because he was more interested in rapid growth than in complacent comfort. Like a heavy elephant, he carried both the weight and wisdom to transform himself again and again, and found the rocky road of entrepreneurship to be an ideal catalyst.

But as summer turned to fall, his vehicle for purpose threatened to stall. As Michael struggled to secure investors, convert customers, and find product-market fit, he grew increasingly dejected and defiant. He had created his company in his own image, and every rejection email or unsuccessful pitch was not only a blow to his bottom line, but a direct assault to his life's purpose. Indeed, he was not just overtaken by the fear of professional failure, but of existential failure, and with work that was infused with so much of *him*—his essence, his intention, his vision for the future—he couldn't understand why others weren't as concerned by the idea of failure. In many ways, he felt that he was responsible for bringing this creation into the world, and he couldn't understand why he'd been given the inspiration to build it, only to have it crumble. In defiance to fate's cruel bait-and-switch, Michael invested more of himself into his work until he had no more to give—he stopped sleeping and eating, began drinking heavily, and his brow began to grow heavier than a late twenty-something-year-old's should. I struggled to pull my elephant out of his muddy funk, and my heart hurt as I watched him sink deeper and deeper into a pit of depression. It felt like nothing short of an actual death when he was forced to shut down his company, and I watched him flail in pain as if the air had been sucked from his lungs.

But as Michael's moodiness was wont to do, his darkness always brought him back around to the light. After a few years of soul-searching and more mainstream meditation than he ever dreamed he'd do, Michael now has a much more *expansive* sense of meaning and purpose. While his melancholy is still an unwavering aspect of his persona—which I hope never changes *too* much—he's accepted that meaning is to be found in every moment, every email, and every forlorn look up at the sky. He now has the embodied knowledge that the path of self-actualization is not a destination but an ongoing journey that demands both a contemplative spirit *and* a joyful one. He allows himself full belly laughs and playful conversation that's profound not because of its intensity, but because of its lightness, and is now on a spontaneous sabbatical exploring the world. Not long ago, he sent me an update about his now brighter entrepreneurial journey: *it's 70 degrees here in Tucson, and I'm currently sitting at one of several juice bars. More yoga studios than people. Going forest bathing on Sunday. And the best tacos I've ever had.* Then he sent a picture of the sun setting over an otherworldly landscape. And I just knowingly smiled.

The Light

Perhaps the ultimate goal of any creator is to activate and express their authentic *self* in its complete wholeness through their work. Indeed, entrepreneurship may be nothing more or less than an accelerated path toward meaning, and it's almost as if entrepreneurial work was designed with the goals of self-actualization in mind: not only does new venture creation allow the Existential Creator to meet their basic needs like money, food, and security, but it can also fulfill their need for self-esteem and self-actualization.[48] Self-actualization rests at the top of Maslow's hierarchy of needs, and has been poetically defined as "man's tendency to actualize himself, to become his potentialities ... to express and activate all the capacities of the organism."[148] While the desire to self-actualize exists within the collective, the urge seems to be at the forefront of the Existential Creator's experience; they possess a nagging desire to not only create something that's valuable, but *of value*. The Existential Creator yearns to be of service in a way that's more than useful, but a profoundly intentional use of the gifts they bring to the world. While the Existential Creator's quest for meaning may be similar in some ways to the passion of the Fiery Creator, the energy of passion is more excitable and impulsive, while meaning is more reflective and, indeed, a touch melancholy. Unlike employees who may struggle to fully express

---

[148] Rogers, C. R. (2016). *On becoming a person: a therapist's view of psychotherapy.* London: Robinson.

themselves through their work, the Existential Creator can transfer the full weight of their spirit into their creations.

Compared to other careers, entrepreneurship is a remarkably potent vehicle for self-actualization with its emphasis on self-expression, creativity, innovation, and non-compliance with the status quo.[149] [150] Entrepreneurial work allows the Existential Creator to translate their own energy—the very essence of who they are—into something that can benefit and be experienced by the collective, and they are motivated by existential yearnings, like finding personal fulfillment, helping society, and achieving independence.[151] The act of creation allows the Existential Creator to express their physical, mental, emotional, and spiritual energy in a way that reflects their fullest potential, and offers them an outlet to express themselves authentically in a form that may very well outlast them. The dream of passing a venture down to future generations is a powerful motivator for the Existential Creator, [152] and they are often driven by the idea that their creation will become their legacy. With the ability to transcend and transform their inner world into something that can be experienced by others, the Existential Creator is not only able to achieve purpose as an individual, but share their purpose with the collective. To use one's own energy and experience to create something of service to others is perhaps the noblest goal of entrepreneurship.

The Existential Creator is often magnetized to entrepreneurial work after they're confronted with an existential fidgeting: they feel as though they're not living up to their fullest potential, and want to transform their energy into something that's not only productive, but a reflection of *who* they are and *how* they want to impact the world.

[149] Tamvada, J. (2010). Entrepreneurship and welfare. *Small Business Economics,* 34(1), 65-79.

[150] Blanchflower, D. G., & Oswald, A. J. (1998). What makes an entrepreneur? *Journal of Labor Economics,* 16(1), 26-60.

[151] Germak, A. J., & Robinson, J. A. (2014). Exploring the motivation of nascent social entrepreneurs. *Journal of Social Entrepreneurship,* 5(1), 5-21.

[152] Alstete, J. W. (2002). On becoming an entrepreneur: an evolving typology. *International Journal of Entrepreneurial Behavior & Research,* 8(4), 222-234.

Traditional employment can be painfully devoid of meaning for the Existential Creator, and they may struggle with feelings of emptiness, apathy, and frustration for years until they find a glimmer of their life's purpose. They crave work in which they can invest their entire heart and spirit, and the pursuit of meaning drives them to seek something that's more than a career, but a destiny. They're instinctively drawn to work that makes them feel fully alive, integrated, and authentic, and this spiritual squirming—a divine calling of sorts—is often so intense it can't be ignored. The decision to become an entrepreneur is often described as a *knowing*, and once the Existential Creator commits to their calling, it can seem far more difficult to *not* pursue it. Once their vision is seen, it can't be unseen. It's as if any other life would be like living in the dark, and for the Existential Creator, it's a path from which they will likely never return.

The Existential Creator who seeks self-actualization often comes across as more of a psychologist, philosopher, poet, sage, or spiritualist than a "businessperson;" they may be less concerned with bottom lines and more concerned with broader impact, and often have a social impact or mission-orientation focus to their work.[151] Almost as if by impulse, the Existential Creator feels it's their God-given responsibility to heal or fix the world, and are often empathetic creators who more closely embody a healer or servant than a warrior or king. While the Existential Creator can sometimes come across as aloof or moody, they are often individuals who tend toward independence, and prefer to open themselves to the people, ideas, and products they deeply love and trust. While the Existential Creator is often accused of being too serious in their willingness to probe the deep questions of existence, this contemplative and introspective nature allows them to better understand their own experience, and in turn, be of service to the world. In fact, this "godliness" among creators is more than just a metaphor, and research has found that entrepreneurs feel closer to God than non-entrepreneurs, are more likely to engage in devotional acts like prayer, and view their non-denominational God as more personal.[153]

---

[153] Dougherty, K. D., Griebel, J., Neubert, M. J., & Park, J. Z. (2013). A religious profile of American entrepreneurs. *Journal for the Scientific Study of Religion*, 52(2), 401-409.

The Dark

But the Existential Creator's path toward meaning doesn't always feel fulfilling. As explored in Chapter 2, entrepreneurs experience depression at significantly higher rates than employees, and while distressing, there's an important, if not imperative, role of this reflective nature. The Existential Creator is not what William James called a "Once Born Soul" who is happy-go-lucky, easygoing, and cares little for the complexities of the world and themselves.[10] Instead, the Existential Creator is more often a "Twice Born Soul" who cares deeply about the nuanced and often dark questions of existence, and is willing to do the highs *and* lows to create a life worth living. It's often *because* of a "crisis of meaning" or "dark night of the soul" that the Existential Creator is drawn to create meaning through entrepreneurial work, and may first suffer through a depressive episode before they realize the way out is through creative, authentic, and meaningful work. While Twice Born Souls are more likely to traverse the depths of experience, it's far from a damning diagnosis; James believed Twice Born Souls are more likely to seek out and achieve a *true* sense of meaning. It's because the Existential Creator sees the world with such clarity and is willing to tolerate discomfort for the sake of growth that they're able to create with such insight and intention. Indeed, James believed depression caused by the loss of meaning should be welcomed, as this is how renewal and rebirth are most readily achieved.

While a crisis isn't necessarily to be feared, it can be helpful for the Existential Creator to be aware of their crisis triggers, as there are many potential crisis points in the process of building, scaling, and selling a venture. While the most obvious crisis point is when a company fails, the Existential Creator can also undergo a crisis if they *succeed*. If the Existential Creator sells or retires from a venture, they may feel as though they've become an irrelevant, unnecessary figure in their own life's purpose. They may also experience a crisis if they grow disengaged with their work because of a change in the scope of responsibilities, like the shift from a founder to a CEO role, or a misalignment between their original vision and the current state of the company, like a strategy change or a transition in the management team. Other triggers include the devolution of a company's culture into one of toxicity and conflict, or the realization that their company, however successful, lacks a sense of meaning or bigger *why*. Indeed, there's often a painful dissonance between what's well-received by consumers and what's well-received by the Existential Creator's spirit. When the Existential Creator realizes they've created an inauthentic or "meaningless" company that's not a reflection of their fullest aspirations and abilities, they are often confronted with the fear of wasting their potential.

While these crisis moments can be used to empower the Existential Creator, allowing them to create with more awareness, they may find themselves too overwhelmed by their night vision to use these lessons as rich learning opportunities. It can be all too easy for the Existential Creator to become lost in the darkness of their experience, and the notion that life lacks meaning has been associated with depression and a myriad of other negative outcomes.[154] The Existential Creator may present as unusually dark and dissatisfied when compared to the sprightly entrepreneurs around them, and possess surprisingly pessimistic views about entrepreneurship, unable to understand how they ever entered it so lightly. With a tendency toward rumination and isolation, the Existential Creator often spends so much time looking *inward* for a sense of meaning that they hide themselves from relationships, activities, and moments of beauty that could fill them back up again. Even the youngest Existential Creators may come across as weathered old souls who have been bruised and battered by the fates, plagued by a harsh inner dialogue that reminds them of the unrespected potential of their spirit. The Existential Creator often tries to hide these struggles, either to maintain a façade of strength or because they feel unworthy of their own suffering, and often feel guilt or shame around their depressive nature. But for the Existential

---

[154] Steger, M. F., Frazier, P., Oishi, S., & Kaler, M. (2006). The meaning in life questionnaire: Assessing the presence of and search for meaning in life. *Journal of counseling psychology*, *53*(1), 80.

Creator, there is no use questioning the validity of their struggles, as their night vision is also what makes them so aware of the light.

To Integrate

The search for meaning is a lifelong process that—in the Existential Creator's eagerness to fulfill their purpose—they may attempt to control. They are often desperate to have a meaningful life *now*, and may fight with their spirit instead of allowing it to show them a fuller way of being. But psychologists, philosophers, and spiritual teachers are of the same mind when they say that meaning is found in every moment, and the simple *belief* that life is meaningful will make it so.[155] So long as the Existential Creator uses their freedom of choice to maintain hope—even in times of suffering and adversity—their life will continue to have meaning. It's essential that the Existential Creator embrace the lessons of their crises, trusting that the depth of their experience is not an indication of brokenness, but of potential. Each and every moment of struggle, confusion, or discontentment is rich topsoil for creative, personal, and professional transcendence, and the most actualized creators aren't the ones who avoid darkness, but who channel their darkness to create light. The challenges of the Existential Creator are not obstacles to happiness, but rather, opportunities *for* happiness.

The Existential Creator can integrate their light and dark by cultivating their capacity for *joy*, even in—or especially in—times of challenge, conflict, and apparent meaninglessness. Meaning is found in *every* moment of living—in times of both bliss and suffering—and life never ceases to have purpose. While the Existential Creator often tries to complicate the quest for meaning, assuming it to be something that must look grand and feel important, they are often surprised to realize that meaning is found in the mundane, the obvious, and the readily available. When the Existential Creator focuses on finding more joy in their work and

---

[155] Frankl, V. E. (1985). *Man's search for meaning.* Simon and Schuster.

life, they experience two-fold relief: meaning is found in moments of joy, and joy lightens the often heavy quest for meaning. While the Existential Creator may spend time fretting about the grandeur of a meaningful life, meaning is more often found in the hiring on an employee, the sharing of wisdom, or the intention to create a company with integrity—it's found in moments of love, creativity, service, beauty, play, and connection. Once the Existential Creator realizes that meaning is infused in every crevice of their life and work, they can trust that fulfillment is not an end goal, but rather a consequence of creating with joy.

- Cultivate deep and meaningful relationships with partners, employees, cofounders, etc.
- Seek out peak experiences marked by ecstasy and beauty, like time in nature or being in love.
- Use humor, lightness, and friendship to take your work less seriously.
- Maintain a perspective of joy, gratitude, awe, and respect for simplicity.
- Practice meditation and mindfulness exercises that instill awareness and presence.
- Reflect on the ways that your challenges have taught you meaningful lessons.
- Recognize the large and small moments in your day that have the potential for meaning.
- Embody the qualities of spontaneity, authenticity, and compassion.
- Cultivate a sense of oneness with humanity and consider how your work benefits the collective.
- Journal on the idea of radical acceptance, acknowledging reality exactly as it is.

Prompts for Deeper Self-Study

- Do you ruminate about the meaning of life? If so, consider how you might incorporate more joy and play into your daily life.

- Do you feel a strong pressure to change the world? If so, consider the ways in which your work is already changing the world.
- Do you tend to isolate yourself? If so, consider how you might invite others into your quest for meaning.
- Do you often feel discouraged by your inability to make an impact? If so, consider how you can start making a small impact on those around you.
- Do you sometimes feel hopeless? If so, consider the notion that you possess the freedom of choice to *choose* hope at any moment.

Recommended reading for the Existential Creator:
Man's Search for Meaning by Viktor Frankl
On Becoming a Person: A Therapist's View of Psychotherapy by Carl Rogers

PART III:
The Way

"The way is within us..."
– C.G. Jung

Chapter 14:
Caring for Complex Wiring

The Resplendent Butterfly

"The contradictions are what make human behavior so maddening and yet so fascinating, all at the same time."
– Joan D. Vinge

On the surface, Pete seemed to be the epitome of a man's man.

An entrepreneur, investor, philanthropist, and beloved professional athlete, Pete exuded a potent warrior energy. From young fans to grown adults, few were unswayed by his captivating magnetism, and Pete seemed to hold the power of countless creators firmly within his muscular, proud chest. His presence wielded an intensity that was palpable from the moment he walked into a room, and he always seemed to have everything under control, which, needless to say, was mighty comforting for investors, employees, and teammates. But after knowing Pete for a few years, I became aware of a different side of his nature: when Pete's armor was down, he exposed a shockingly gentle spirit. Though his social media followers or opponents might not have sensed it, Pete possessed many soft, creative, and, dare I say, archetypally feminine qualities. Behind the scenes, I knew him to be an artist, philosopher, and explorer, as well as a selfless son, brother, and friend, and I hoped that one day, the world would have the honor of seeing the gentler side of Pete's nature.

Little did I know, that day would come sooner than expected. One afternoon, on his widely followed social media account, he shared a post in support of women's empowerment. His caption summarized his deep admiration for women, and was a call for empathy and inclusion. A knowing smile spread across my face and I immediately liked the post, but as I began scrolling through an increasingly long list of comments, my heart sank. Slack-jawed, I read the brutal commentary left on his post by boys as young as 12 years old. They tore into his soft message, and threatened to unfollow his account in utter disappointment of his "weakness" and "sensitivity." Perhaps his post appeared to be in stark contrast to many of his "stronger" qualities, and while I wasn't surprised that he would share such a message, it was clearly an affront to many of his fans who wanted to view him as a tough, masculine creator. After a day of harassment, I quite expected Pete to be distressed and perhaps regretful, so I typed up a message to express my appreciation.

Much to my surprise, Pete was not only unshaken by the blowback, but proceeded to lean into his wholeness even more. From that day forward, his posts frequently showcased his thoughtful emotions, contemplative stances, colorful wardrobe, and playful bits of hand-painted artwork. In beautiful and bursting synchrony, Pete began to hold and display his multitudes like the most resplendent butterfly, and I relished watching him merge his multitudes. He simultaneously displayed his masculine and feminine, logical and creative, and aggressive and nurturing qualities, and while he embodied the energy of a warrior and king on the field, he just as readily embodied the energy of an artisan, scholar, and servant in his work. Pete didn't fight with the many creators within his being—the creators who wanted to teach, speak, play, lead, and innovate—because he came to view them as one in the same. He gave all of his inner muses fresh air to breathe, and as a result, they thrived. I believe Pete realized that he had a responsibility to lean into the many creators within his being for the benefit of all, and knew that he wasn't serving himself or his fans by conforming to the expectations of how a creator *should* be.

By weaving together all of the most dissonant aspects of his personality, Pete became a true force of creative nature, and offered something to the world that no one else could. His work came directly from his spirit—uniquely and unapologetically—and that was a competitive advantage that no one could challenge. But admittedly, at the time I met Pete, I was still working through many of these lessons myself. I had worked for the past few years on reconciling my light and dark, but was still struggling to understand how I could weave together my most dissonant interests and qualities: emotion and logic, mysticism and science, humor and seriousness, femininity and masculinity, and the like. I was already far along the path of loving my own complexities, but I still believed that I wouldn't be accepted by others if I stood in my messiness as a creator: *how will I explain myself to people? Am I allowed to be all of this?* I feared that I would be perceived as too much, too little, or too confusing. And this was the precious gift that Pete gave me: as I watched him embrace his wholeness—confidently standing in and showcasing his glorious contradiction—I was inspired to do the same. I realized that I had to declare my wholeness, without insecurity or hesitation, if I was to honor my potential as a conduit for creation.

And so, I began the process of embodying and expressing my multitudes, not only in the confines of my apartment, but in front of the world. I began playing with the boundaries of my public authenticity, and came to quickly learn that the more I showed of myself, the more I attracted the people, opportunities, and resources I needed to send my message out into the world. While I had never more "unfollowed" than in this transition to vulnerability and self-love, I had also never been more validated by those whose feedback and support I truly respected. It quickly became clear that embracing my multitudes didn't just feel good in my own skin, but allowed me to create more efficiently and potently than I ever knew possible. I realized that embodying my fullness didn't just benefit me as an individual, but it benefited the precious creation that I had been entrusted to deliver to the world.

And, perhaps for the first time, both Pete *and* I were truly ready to hold it all.

> *"The most terrifying thing is to accept oneself completely."*
> – C.G. Jung

Creating from Wholeness

"The curious paradox is that when I accept myself just as I am,
then I can change."
– Carl R. Rogers

At this point, I hope the message is self-evident: to become a clearer conduit for creation, entrepreneurial spirits must counterintuitively wade into their muddiness first. They must align themselves with every contradiction, cherish every nuance, and celebrate every flaw. For creators, the process of embracing their multitudes requires them to take intimate stock of their depths, becoming curious about the parts of themselves they readily discard so that they can use *all* of themselves to create. No part of a creator is ugly, shameful, or inconvenient. No part of them is an unworthy source of inspiration for their work. An entrepreneur's complexity is their greatest competitive advantage, and their fulfillment won't be found in the simplification of their experience, but in learning how to integrate the complexity of their wiring. The process of creating is a hero's journey, and shadowy parts of a creator will inevitably emerge over their career; however, as they learn to integrate their light and dark, they will find that their battles no longer turn into wars, and they will be able to find solutions faster with much more grace and ease. In coming to know themselves, creators will be better able to regulate the tension of their light and dark, and honor all of the creators within their being who demand an outlet for expression.

Carrying forth the knowledge from the previous chapters, readers may be asking themselves: *now what? How do I create a path forward?* There is no right or wrong way to engage in ongoing self-study, as the term quite literally offers the power back to the individual. What's quite delightful about the process of embracing one's multitudes is that it does not *necessitate* the participation of therapists, coaches, guides, and healers. While I'm the first to admit that a wise guide can be instrumental in the process of self-study, I'm also a firm believer that creators should never feel as though they *must* outsource this journey. The guidance of others can provide a useful mirror, but it can do little more than that, and a real teacher will never say that the answers can only be found through working with them. It's important that creators are mindful of the way they give their power to others, and understand that the process of coming home to the creative self is fundamentally an *inward* journey.

While there is no *one* way to understand oneself, there are a collection of tools, techniques, and practices that can facilitate this process. It's in each creator's hands to decide which practices resonate most for them, but for those readers who would like a more formal process, I recommend completing the exercise below. To do this, choose one, several or all of the archetypes that resonate, and create a map for further self-study. A simple map outline is as follows, including an example of my map for the Orderly Creator:

I am the _____ Creator
Example: I am the Orderly Creator

- **Self-Understanding:** How do you embody the dark qualities of this archetype? How does this negatively affect you?
    - **Example:** *I have controlling patterns in both work and life. These perfectionistic tendencies cause me to fuss about things that I can't change, and make it hard for me to trust myself and others.*
- **Self-Acceptance:** How can you draw a line between the dark and light qualities of this archetype? How are your struggles also your strengths?
    - **Example:** *I realize that these controlling tendencies stem from my conscientiousness which is also the source of my diligence and organization. Without my conscientiousness, this book wouldn't exist, nor would I have achieved early success in my career.*
- **Self-Care:** How can you integrate the dark and light qualities of this archetype? What tools, practices, or techniques (in the book or otherwise) will you use to regulate this archetype?
    - **Example:** *To ease my hyper-conscientious tendencies, I will create a daily meditation, reflection, and movement practice that helps deepen my capacity for trust, surrender, and acceptance. I acknowledge my belief that everything happens for a reason, and will remind myself: all is well.*

This practice can be repeated for several or all archetypes, and will help draw a line between one's light and dark qualities. Though this process is simple, it's a powerful tool to reframe one's struggles as strengths, and appreciate one's depths as the source of one's greatest potential.

"I am as bad as the worst, but, thank God, I am as good as the best. "
– *Walt Whitman*

A Richer Toolbelt

"I am more and more interested in the interaction between oneself and others and in the technologies of individual domination, the history of how an individual acts upon himself, in the technology of self."
— *Michel Foucault*

Today's culture is rife with quick fixes, and some creators may be tempted to invest in superficial pathways that promise greater productivity, influence, and happiness. While these offerings may provide some useful frameworks, they will consistently and frustratingly fail if they do not also provide a foundation of self-study. At the end of the day, no leadership training or performance coach will make a lasting impact if they aren't rooted solidly in practices of self-understanding, self-acceptance, and sustainable self-care. While some may find issue with this book because there are no prescriptions, precise regimens, or 30-day cures, I've found these approaches to be largely ineffective, particularly for the entrepreneurial spirit. In all of my interactions with creators, the single most empowering piece of knowledge I can provide is a framework for self-study. When creators are empowered to identify where a certain feeling, desire, motivation, or behavior comes from, they're often able to integrate the lesson and reconcile the imbalance without fussy techniques and expensive trainings. It's remarkable how quickly creators can come home to themselves once they obtain an awareness of the *root* of their struggles, and it often takes nothing more than giving a thing a name for it to lose its power. I may be putting myself out of the job with this notion, but I believe that creators can reconcile even their most startling contradictions once they draw their attention inward, confronting their complex and exquisite selves with the utmost empathy.

What this book *does* offer is what is called "technologies of self." The late philosopher Michel Foucault was the first to use the term, and defined it as any practice that brings an individual closer to a state of wholeness, balance, and integration.[156] Distinct from technologies of production, sign systems, and power, technologies of self are practices that concern the self, with the intent of knowing and

> ## Technologies of Self
>
> "Permit individuals to effect by their own means or with the help of others a certain number of operations on their own souls, thoughts, conduct, and way of being, so as to transform themselves in order to attain a certain state of happiness, purity, wisdom, perfection, or immortality."

taking care of the self. In Foucault's famous essay on the subject, he explores common technologies of self over the centuries like prayer, writing, dream analysis, dialogue, and other forms of self-examination, and concludes that it's the greatest and most important lesson in life to know oneself. Importantly, these technologies of self require little if any participation from the external world, and allow the individual to explore their own depths without deference to a third-party. The following technologies of self were frequently recommended throughout the book, and are worth exploring on the path of self-study:

- **Meditation:** The practice of training the mind's awareness for an improved sense of presence and calm. Common types of meditation include mindfulness meditation, Zen meditation, transcendental meditation, loving-kindness meditation, visualization meditation, and more.

---

[156] Foucault, M., Martin, L. H., Gutman, H., & Hutton, P. H. (1988). *Technologies of the self: a seminar with Michel Foucault.* Amherst: University of Massachusetts Press.

- **Nature:** The practice of spending time outdoors with the intention of calming, grounding, and inspiring. Common examples include forest bathing, hiking, swimming, running, climbing, gardening, and more.
- **Breathwork:** The practice of regulating the breath to create and activate a calming parasympathetic response in the body and mind. Common types of breathwork include equal breathing, box breathing, abdominal breathing, alternate nostril breathing, kapalabhati breathing, and more.
- **Journaling:** The practice of writing down one's thoughts and feelings without inhibition, guidance, or structure. Common types of journaling include reflecting on one's day, past, future, goals, dreams, challenges, gratitude, and more.
- **Yoga Asana:** The practice of moving the body through a series of postures that create an alignment of the mind, body, and spirit. Common types of yoga include Vinyasa, Bikram, Hatha, Iyengar, Kundalini, Ashtanga, Yin, Dharma, Prana, Restorative, Jivamukti, and more.
- **Bodywork:** The practice of adjusting, manipulating, stretching, and relaxing the body to create a state of health. Common types of bodywork include acupuncture, acupressure, myofascial release, trigger point therapy, craniosacral therapy, reiki, cupping, and more.
- **Prayer and mantras:** The practice of connecting with a higher power, including one's higher self, through an act of devotion. Common examples include prayers, intentions, affirmations, mantras, and more.

"It is not the length of life, but the depth."
— *Ralph W. Emerson*

Addressing the Ecosystem

"The Self is a union of opposites par excellence...."
– C.G. Jung

The time has come for the entrepreneurial ecosystem to stop glorifying imbalance and condoning dis-ease for the sake of creation. It's an antiquated if not barbaric way of creating, and has consequences not just for the individual creator, but for the impact they have on society. A creation will always reflect the health of its creator, and if we all wish to live in a healthier society, we must invest at the source. To bring the ecosystem forward into a state of consciousness and intentionality, I urge creators to carry these lessons into their companies and cultures, making self-study an *imperative*, and teach others that they must commit to the inspection and maintenance of their own vessel just as rigorously as they would their companies. While there is much that an entrepreneur can achieve on their own, their efforts will only go so far if key stakeholders in the entrepreneurial ecosystem maintain an archaic approach—perpetuating toxic masculinity, stoicism, gratuitous celebrations of power, unrealistic metrics of success, and the like—to creation. Like nature, the entrepreneurial ecosystem is deeply connected and intertwined, and when one aspect is cared for, the rest of the ecosystem will inevitably benefit. To that end, I will briefly touch on the various ways that the whole ecosystem can be brought into this conversation:

- **Company Cultures:** It has become a popular trend to offer luxe perks of employment within entrepreneurial workplaces in an effort to improve employee wellness, like unlimited vacation days and in-house masseuses. While these well-meaning offerings address the self-care aspect of self-study, they do little if anything to help employees address the deeper roots of any struggles they may face. Instead of focusing resources on these "band-aids," companies could turn their focus to creating workplace cultures that are characterized by vulnerability, authenticity, and a dedication to ongoing personal growth. This may take the form of a self-study program, peer support group, more intimate relationship between employees and the executive team, designated coach or therapist, or another offering along these lines.

- **Universities:** Students are perhaps my favorite group to work with, as they're at an ideal point to learn the tools of self-study that will benefit them once they enter the workplace. However, while many universities offer some kind of entrepreneurship class, program, or department, the instruction is still largely based on building a business. Not only does this make students ill-prepared for the personal challenges they will inevitably encounter, but may leave them with a rosy or idealized view of entrepreneurship. To address this, universities may consider working with their psychology or other wellness-focused department to craft a course specifically around the *human* experience of new venture creation. A shining example of this is Georgetown's Entrepreneurship Initiative, a program infused with the university's Jesuit value of cura *personalis*—a Latin phrase meaning "care for the entire person." By offering curriculum and programs that focus on the whole person—mental, emotional, physical, and spiritual—Georgetown has been able to secure not only the professional success of their graduates, but personal success as well.

- **Investors:** In defense of the investment community, there has not been a well-articulated incentive for investors to not only invest in companies, but also in the well-being of their portfolio founders. Currently, it doesn't behoove an investor to take the stance of: *make slow and steady progress. Take good care of yourself.* This will require the ecosystem to creatively explore how to create aligned incentives for investors and portfolio founders. In other words, how can it be a win-win for creators *and* investors if companies are built in a mentally, physically, emotionally, and spiritually sustainable way? How can it be financially fruitful to incorporate founder well-being into a firm's investment thesis?

- **Incubators, Accelerators & Mentorship Programs:** The structure of most incubator and accelerator programs is admittedly designed to be combustive. In a matter of weeks or months, creators are expected to produce viable companies, and those who aren't "fit" are weeded out. This Darwinian approach to creation, while perhaps understandable in its intent, can wreak havoc on the wellness of the participants. Beyond providing self-study resources for participants, these programs may consider a structure that allows for more spaciousness and intentionality. At a higher level, they may also consider if it's in anyone's best interest—*including* the program or fund itself—for these companies to be built at such a breakneck pace.

- **Governments:** Admittedly, the interaction between entrepreneurship and government remains a bit of a black box for me. While I have yet to fully understand the nuances of advocacy, policy, government funding, and the like, I know enough to pose this question to those with greater fluency: how can the case be made that the well-being of creators has direct societal, cultural, and economic ramifications? How can issues like sustainability, corruption, and greed be tied back to the intentionality of creators? How can it be made clear that investing in creators as individuals is a national imperative?

"I exist as I am, that is enough."
– *Walt Whitman*

Wired This Way

"Contradiction is the essence of the universe."
– *Fernando Pessoa*

Dear creator,

We are coming to the end of our journey together, and if you close this book feeling even the slightest bit in awe of yourself, then we both have succeeded. More important than perhaps anything else is that you are kind to yourself as you navigate the path of self-study. You were not born incorrectly, and you most certainly aren't irreconcilably bad, but neither do you have to be perfect to be a whole creator. To come into lasting state of wholeness, you must acknowledge and accept every single wire in your system—every complexity, contradiction, dissonance, and shadow that you believe to be your greatest, ugliest, and most damning flaw—and integrate them into one spectacular whole. The richness of being that will come from this process is the same richness seen in so many great creators across history, and this profundity of self comes only when you accept each part of your whole. The process of integration is not a process of eliminating your unproductive qualities, but of recognizing that every quality—light and dark—stems from the same source as your brilliance. It's not a question of simplifying, but of consolidating. It's not a process of sacrificing, but of harmonizing. It's not a matter of becoming less, but of becoming an expansive whole. It's all you—and you have to use *all* of it to create.

There is nothing wrong with you.
You are just wired this way.

> *"Do I contradict myself? Very well then I contradict myself,*
> *(I am large, I contain multitudes.)"*
> — *Walt Whitman*

Afterword

Entrepreneurs Are Vulnerable; Buffering Entrepreneurship Benefits Everyone

Michael A. Freeman, MD, Clinical Professor of Psychiatry, UCSF School of Medicine & Mentor, The Entrepreneurship Center at UCSF

Most people are not entrepreneurs. From a mainstream perspective, these distinctive business builders, with their hair-raising brand of mission-driven, bet-the-farm adventurism, can seem like a different breed. Yet while these millionaires and thrillionaires may be difficult to relate to and seem so unlike you and me, entrepreneurs are people too. They have strengths and foibles, courage and insecurities, hopes and fears, dreams and regrets, wins and setbacks, and an embarrassing propensity to mess things up—in fact, just like the rest of us. Within that context, Jessica Carson helps us to understand that entrepreneurs are not only people, but people who matter. And they are people who can benefit from our empathy and support as well as self-care skills and public policies that buffer the blows of entrepreneurship. Since they suffer and derail as a result of the same forces that empower them to succeed, it behooves us to facilitate their personal growth and development while they, in turn, facilitate our economic growth and development.

Wired This Way is intended for entrepreneurs and for the universe of people whose intimate engagement with them helps them succeed. It suggests that loved ones, coaches, investors, peers, therapists and team members can learn to look past the wealth and wipeouts, the notoriety and charisma, the humiliations and achievements, and engage more fully. Like the products that entrepreneurs create, Jessica Carson iterates her way through *Wired This Way* toward her unique formulation of a path to wellness and wholeness for entrepreneurs.

Today, for the first time, we are getting to know entrepreneurs as people by hearing from founders and their loved ones directly in their unfiltered, uninterpreted, authentic voices. Entrepreneurs are beginning to tell their own stories with voices with tones that can be, at times, plaintive, proud, frightened, determined, distraught and bold. These are stories that express their personalities, share their mental health issues, and present the narratives of their triumphs and tragedies. We are discovering these stories in books like *Killing It* by Sheryl O'Loughlin, *Option B* by Sheryl Sandberg and Adam Grant, *Copy This* by Paul Orfalea, *Startup Life* by Brad Feld and Amy Batchelor, and *The Hard Thing about Hard Things* by Ben Horowitz; in podcasts like *How I Built It* and *Zen Founder*; and in innumerable emphatic blog posts that twinkle and shimmer in the vast expanse of cyberspace.

Recognizing that entrepreneurs are people may seem self-evident to entrepreneurs, and to those who have read *Wired This Way* by Jessica Carson. Nonetheless, the entrepreneurship research, education, policy and services establishment has been slow to embrace the centrality of this premise. Economists, for example, do not identify entrepreneurs as inspired individuals who overcome early life adversity only to enter an adulthood defined by emotional extremes. Instead, they define entrepreneurs by what they do rather than who they are.

Economists posit that entrepreneurs are economic actors who drive the engines of capitalist production, and conveyors of "animal spirits"[157] into inefficient markets. They see entrepreneurs as agents of commerce who foment creative destruction as they detect and exploit market opportunities. Entrepreneurs are viewed as disruptive, ingenious, risk-taking innovators who create value by coordinating relationships between inventors, producers, investors and consumers.[158] The fate of those who fail – the majority – is often of little concern to economists because who actually cares

---

[157] Dow, A. & Dow, S. (2011). Animal Spirits Revisited. *Capitalism and Society*, 6(2), published on line. doi:10.2202/1932-0213.1087

[158] Fomaini, Robert L. (2001). The engine of capitalist process: entrepreneurs in economic theory. *Economic and Financial Review*, Federal Reserve Bank of Dallas, Fourth Quarter, 2001, pp. 1-11. https://www.dallasfed.org/~/media/documents/research/efr/2001/efr0104a.pdf

about individual entrepreneurs and the agonizing anxiety they face on their journeys along the economic superhighway to a future that may not include them?

In the eyes of many academics and policymakers, entrepreneurs are defined by the utility they provide. The utilitarian position is that entrepreneurs are actors and agents, innovators and disruptors, opportunity finders and profit seekers, job creators, and prosperity builders whose output can be amplified by innovation policy. Maybe. But perhaps all these attributes are reflections of something more basic, namely, that entrepreneurs are people with a unique way of doing things; people who have hopes and dreams, issues and concerns, strengths and vulnerabilities, and complicated lives of their own. When they pursue their hopes and dreams, when they live their lives and address their issues, useful social and economic impacts can be extracted if the policy parameters are properly set. However the adverse personal consequences accrue primarily to the entrepreneurs themselves, and then radiate out like aftershocks and ripples that spread across the communities and ecosystems in which they operate and the families in which they live.

While the social utility of entrepreneurs was initially recognized by the French economist Richard Cantillon in the mid-1700s,[174] [159] it took more than 250 years for economists to start thinking about entrepreneurs as people who, despite their supernova qualities, are very real human beings with personalities and mental health issues of their own. In 2007 the German investigators Andreas Rauch and Michel Frese recognized that the personality of entrepreneurs relates directly to their success, and declared, "Let's put the person back into entrepreneurship research";[160] since that time the personality traits of entrepreneurs have been clearly identified by

---

[159] Spengler, Joseph J. (1960), "Richard Cantillon: First of the Moderns," in *Essays in Economic Thought: Aristotle to Marshall*, ed. J. J. Spengler and W. R. Allen, 2nd ed. (Chicago: Rand McNally), pp. 105–40.
[160] Rauch, A. & M. Frese. (2007). Let's put the person back into entrepreneurship research: A meta-analysis on the relationship between business owners' personality traits, business creation, and success. *European Journal of Work and Organizational Psychology*, 16, 353-385.

an avalanche of scientific research. Hundreds of careful studies confirm that characteristics such as openness to experience, extraversion, industriousness, need for autonomy, self-efficacy, risk propensity and the like are forces that shape the lives of entrepreneurs.[161] Furthermore, a separate research stream confirms that personality traits are genetically transmitted and environmentally shaped in equal measure.[162] Thus appreciating that entrepreneurs are people and that people are part of nature has helped us begin to understand that the engine of capitalist production is, to a significant degree, biological, genetically transmitted, and ancestral in origin.

This recognition has inspired a new generation of scholars to investigate the evolutionary, psychological and brain-based dimensions of entrepreneurship in search of the animal behind the animal spirits. Noting that traits associated with bipolar disorder (such as sociability, intelligence, energy, and goal engagement) confer adaptive advantage[163] in ways that benefit entrepreneurs, my colleagues and I explored the prevalence and co-occurrence of mental health conditions among entrepreneurs and their family members.[164] We identified a profile of entrepreneurial strengths (such as persistence and endurance powered by high energy and decreased need for sleep), and vulnerabilities (such as impulsivity, recklessness and distractibility powered by an elevated need for stimulation and chaos) that are related to mental health conditions

---

[161] Kerr, S.P., Kerr, W. R., & Xu, T. (2018). Personality traits of entrepreneurs: a review of recent literature. *Foundations and Trends in Entrepreneurship*, vol. 14, no. 3, pp. 279–356, ISBN: 978-1-68083-449-9

[162] Bouchard, Thomas J., Jr. (2004) Genetic influence on human psychological traits, a survey. *Current Directions in Psychological Science*, vol. 13, no. 4, pp. 148-151. https://doi.org/10.1111/j.0963-7214.2004.00295.x

[163] Higier, R.G., Jimenez, A.M., Hultman, C.M., Borg, J., Roman, C., Kizling, I., Larsson, H., Cannon, T. D. (2014). Enhanced neurocognitive functioning and positive temperament in twins discordant for bipolar disorder. *American Journal of Psychiatry*, Nov. 2014, Vol. 171, pp. 1191-1198. https://doi.org/10.1176/appi.ajp.2014.13121683

[164] Freeman, M.A., Staudenmaier, P.J., Zisser, M.R. et al. (2019). The prevalence and co-occurrence of psychiatric conditions among entrepreneurs and their families. *Small Business Economics* 53: 323-342. https://doi.org/10.1007/s11187-018-0059-8

which are commonly experienced by founders and co-founders. In this study and others, our group and our international colleagues have consistently found that these conditions, symptoms, and sub-threshold temperaments shape the social, emotional, cognitive, and behavioral dimensions of the lived experience, business results, and personal life outcomes of entrepreneurs.

As early as 1993, investigators began to recognize the relationship between specific conditions like ADHD, and entry into entre-preneurship.[165] Today, investigators around the world are studying the importance of the strengths, and also the vulnerabilities that entrepreneurs obtain as a result of clinical and sub-threshold expression of bipolar spectrum conditions, depression, anxiety, substance and behavioral addictions, and ADHD. Among these contemporary scholars, a new and person-based economic perspective has begun to emerge. Simply stated, converging lines of evidence indicate that innovation, growth, and prosperity are not possible without the co-occurrence of clinically significant mental health conditions. Businesses effervesce from the cauldron of mental health differences like bubbles that effervesce from a glass of champagne. A new clinical perspective is emerging as well. Carefully crafted therapy and mental health-informed coaching, based on a granular and sophisticated understanding of the human factor dimensions of entrepreneurship, may help entrepreneurs build upon their strengths while mitigating the suffering and career derailments that can result from the intrusion of intense and extreme emotional and behavioral states.

The minds of entrepreneurs can thus be understood as a modern reflection of an ancient strain of neurodiversity; a strain that manifests the neural and psychological plasticity[166] that has powered

---

[165] Mannuzza, S., Klein, R.G., Bessler, A. Malloy, P., LaPadula, M.A. (1993). Adult outcome of hyperactive boys; educational achievement, occupational rank, and psychiatric status. *Archives of General Psychiatry* vol. 50, July 1993, pp. 565-576. doi:10.1001/archpsyc.1993.01820190067007

[166] DeYoung, C. G. (2006). Higher-order factors of the Big Five in a multi-infor-mant sample. *Journal of Personality and Social Psychology*, 91(6), 1138-1151. http://dx.doi.org/10.1037/0022-3514.91.6.1138

our astonishing evolution. Genetically transmitted and environmentally shaped personality traits, brain-based and environmentally triggered temperaments and mental health symptoms, in the context of creativity, innovation, improvisation, proactivity and adaptation in the service of value creation and economic growth are increasingly construed as part of the same human plot line.

Upon reflection, this should not be a surprise. From a distance, entrepreneurs may be recognized as members of a unique evolutionary tribe that inhabits the leading edge of a vast mythopoetic story arc. The arc of this legend extends across an epoch that spans the last 500,000 years. From the dawn of our pre-human ancestors to the emergence of early post-humans in the 21st century,[167] people with the propensity for entrepreneurship have been breaking rules, disrupting the status quo, discovering opportunities and leading migrations from places we long ago forgot to places we cannot yet imagine.[168] [169] [170] [171]

The contours of this plot line, however, may elude recognition by entrepreneurs themselves. Unaware of their evolutionary heritage, immersed in the wow of the now, passionate, hopeful, enthralled, frustrated, terrified and burned out, entrepreneurs experience the urgency of the present and envision the possibility of the near future as they build a lasting legacy that exceeds their imaginations.

---

[167] Harari, Y.N. (2016). *Homo Deus; a Brief History of Tomorrow*. Vintage, Penguin Random House U.K. ISBN 9781784703936

[168] Ashraf, Q. & Galor, O. (2013). The 'Out of Africa' hypothesis, human genetic diversity, and comparative economic development. *American Economic Review*. 2013 February ; 103(1): 1–46.

[169] Li, W-D., Wang, N., Arvey, R.D., Soong, R., Mei Saw, S., and Song, Z. (2015). A mixed blessing? Dual mediating mechanisms in the relationship between dopamine transporter gene DAT1 and leadership role occupancy. *The Leadership Quarterly* Volume 26, Issue 5, October 2015, Pages 671-686.

[170] Harari, Y.N. (2016). *Homo Deus; a Brief History of Tomorrow*. Vintage, Penguin Random House U.K. ISBN 9781784703936

[171] Ebstein, R.P., Novick, O., Umansky, R., Priel, B., Osher, Y., Blaine, D., Bennett, E.R., Nemarov, L., Katz, M., Belmaker, R.H. (1996). Dopamine D4 receptor (D4DR) exon III polymorphism associated with the human personality trait of Novelty Seeking. *Nature Genetics*, Vol. 12, pp 78-80 (1996)

Rather than accommodating the world as it is, they imagine the world that could be and push forward relentlessly as they strive to create it. At close range, creative destruction, disruption of inefficient markets, and channeling animal spirits into the pressing priorities of everyday life results in a riot of all-consuming, somewhat-controlled chaos for individual entrepreneurs.

Since entrepreneurs are people, those of us who care about them may set aside utilitarian characterizations and endeavor to understand them more empathically by listening as they express their lived experience in their own words. Open-minded and open-hearted listening has the potential to vastly enrich both the field of entrepreneurship and the economic theory that guides prosperity-centric macroeconomic policy. This kind of listening also helps the people who support entrepreneurs to develop founder-centric strength building and risk reduction strategies in order to help prevent career derailment and avoidable pain and suffering among the people who drive economic growth.

For example, understanding and empathizing with the lived experience of actual entrepreneurs can teach us to refrain from stigmatizing and penalizing people with the propensity for entrepreneurship because they are different. As Salvatore Mannuzza and his colleagues showed us in 1993, the entrepreneurs of tomorrow are sitting in the back rows of middle school classrooms today, chewing gum, chatting it up, throwing paper airplanes, making funny noises when the teachers aren't looking, and being sent to detention for disrupting classrooms and breaking rules. Let's face it; entrepreneurs are not simply different. From the perspective of the establishment, in their early years they are often viewed as misfits, trouble makers, and unemployable rule breakers within the context of cultures built by those who prefer tradition, pre-dictability, stability and order. By the time they become adults, many of them have been emotionally injured by the incessant criticism and the recurring contempt dished out by authorities who can see what is wrong with them but lack the neutrality and peripheral vision to see what is right with them.[181] [172] [173] [174]

However, cultures created by the guardians of the status quo can stagnate for centuries, resulting in dark ages in which not much happens and little is new. Progress is contingent upon innovation, and hence requires disruption. Thus the guardians of the status quo must eventually turn to entrepreneurs. Ironically, in the eyes of others, disrupting classrooms and household tranquility is bad but disrupting the economy and market tranquility is good. From the entrepreneur's perspective, how does that make sense? From pre-adolescence to young adulthood not much has changed for these restless explorers who chafe at the constraints of the world they were born into, but for some reason as adults they now have a lot more friends. They are no longer being sent to detention and are attracting investors instead.

In the folklore of entrepreneurship, entrepreneurs are the B students and dropouts who hire the A students and valedictorians. The very same people are both rejected as juvenile delinquents or admired as economic heroes; stigmatized as unbalanced wildcards or lauded as visionary leaders. Another option is available to guardians of the status quo who nonetheless depend upon disruption. We can all learn to accept and embrace both dimensions of the entrepreneurial psyche in a way that normalizes these individual differences. This formulation lends itself to mutually strengthening the economy and the people who build it by offering the kind of support that improves both the business outcomes and the life outcomes of entrepreneurs.

---

[172] Zhang, Z., Arvey, R.D. (2009). Rule breaking in adolescence and entrepreneurial status: An empirical investigation. *Journal of Business Venturing* Vol. 24, No. 5, Sept. 2009, Pages 436-447 https://doi.org/10.1016/j.jbusvent.2008.04.009

[173] Levine, R., Rubinstein, Y. (2017). Smart and illicit: Who becomes an entrepreneur and do they earn more?, *The Quarterly Journal of Economics*, Vol. 132, Issue 2, May 2017, Pages 963-1018, https://doi.org/10.1093/qje/qjw044

[174] Obschonka, M., Andersson, H., Silbereisen, R.K., Sverke, M., (2013). Rule-breaking, crime, and entrepreneurship: A replication and extension study with 37-year longitudinal data *Journal of Vocational Behavior*, Vol. 83, No. 3, Dec. 2013, Pages 386-396. https://doi.org/10.1016/j.jvb.2013.06.007

On a parallel track, therapists and coaches who work with entrepreneurs as people have begun to fill out the picture and look for ways to buffer the adverse impact of the entrepreneurial journey. Books like *The Hypomanic Edge* by John Gartner, *Born to Build* by Sangeeta Badal and Jim Clifton, and *Reboot* by Jerry Colonna have begun to share a humanistic, entrepreneur-centric, wellness-focused and mental health-informed view of entrepreneurs as people. This is where Jessica Carson's book, *Wired This Way*, provides insight. Jessica describes her personal journey, shaped by many of the same forces that shape the lives of entrepreneurs, and the understanding she gleaned into how entrepreneurs can enhance their strengths and personality highlights, minimize the dark side of these same traits, and mitigate the slings and arrows of their outrageous fortune.

Jessica shares her story and insights with the excitement of someone who has discovered that entrepreneurs are people who matter. Why do they matter? Here's what she says in Chapter 1 of *Wired This Way*: "Creators have an enormous impact on the development of humankind at a global scale, and the mental, emotional, physical, and spiritual well-being of entrepreneurs isn't just a concern for entrepreneurs—it's a concern for humanity. Entrepreneurship is at the heart of social and economic growth, and is responsible for everything from job creation to social trends to the adoption of new technologies by the collective.[175] Entrepreneurial spirits create the next version of reality for *all* of us, and if the source code isn't functioning properly, there's little hope for the end result. While every human is responsible for leaving their mark on this world, entrepreneurial spirits are often the ones who do so at scale and therefore have the potential to leave a largest impact—positive *or* negative. Recent news has been littered with examples of creators behaving "badly"—and these failings, while personal, also have an impact on the broader social, cultural, and economic landscape. It's in the best interest of everyone in the entrepreneurial ecosystem

---

[175] Van Praag, C. M., & Versloot, P. H. (2007). What is the value of entrepreneurship? A review of recent research. *Small business economics, 29*(4), 351-382.

like investors, universities, government, and other stakeholders to invest in the fountainhead of the creative process: the entrepreneur.

"By investing in the well-being of creators, we invest in the future of humanity. If we want to create a happy and healthy future, we must ensure the designers of that future are happy and healthy too. The ability to influence global trends is not a responsibility to be taken lightly, and I believe that all entrepreneurs should be as eagerly armed with the tools to take care of themselves as they are their companies. By encouraging the development of self-awareness in entrepreneurs, they will inevitably create products that reflect this heightened awareness, and when we support their well-being, we ensure the integrity of the impact they leave on the collective. Creators are patient zero of our modern day breakthroughs and epidemics—they are the parents from which all creations and their consequences are born. If key stakeholders begin to see the individual creator as this most critical starting point, they will inevitably be compelled to shift their investment strategy: instead of investing in products once they are already built, they might begin to see value in investing at the source. Elevating the intentionality of products is a nice goal, but is a rather clumsy and inefficient effort when the ecosystem could be elevating the consciousness of the creators themselves."

This points to a new kind of shared prosperity. Most startups fail but some do succeed. In the process of failing or succeeding, most entrepreneurs get pounded by turbulent emotional whitewater and unforeseen traumatic blows as they persistently press forward. Fear, uncertainty, frustration, distress, doubt, grief and exhaustion are in abundant supply. According to Jessica, it doesn't have to be that hard. With the right personal growth tools, entrepreneurs and the community they serve can have a lot more gain and a lot less emotional pain.

Contemporary entrepreneurship has accelerated the rate of change in virtually every sphere of life. The need for tools and resources to help entrepreneurs gain and maintain balance and perspective in this context could not be more pressing because many social welfare burdens have inadvertently landed on their shoulders. policymakers cannot keep up with this rate of change and the impact of innovation upon the societies they are entrusted to guide. Without the external resources required to learn how to regulate extreme emotions and develop broader contextual appreciation, and without the role models required to develop wisdom that transcends the thrill of achieving short-term goals, entrepreneurs may be challenged to fully own and help to protect the future that they are helping to create.

As if that weren't enough, it increasingly falls to the entrepreneurs themselves to understand and speak up about the social, cultural, and political impact that results from the innovations they introduce. How are entrepreneurs supposed to anticipate and cope with the ways in which their innovations can be weaponized? How can the marginalized misfits who find their way into changing the world maintain the equanimity required to establish guardrails that keep innovation on track? Since the rate of innovation so exceeds public policy lag time, and since innovation has proven easy to co-opt by those with malicious intent, entrepreneurs must now provide a higher level of utility, for which they are developmentally, conceptually and emotionally poorly prepared. Providing the resources they need to succeed is a move in the right direction. Getting from here to there is not easy and the path forward is not entirely clear.

However, the likelihood of success is greater if you start somewhere, learn something, and improve. This is what Jessica Carson chose to do in her book, *Wired This Way*. A broad community of interest must collaborate to build out the solutions that Jessica's book suggests. That's OK, because solutions emerge in successive iterations informed by stakeholder feedback that builds engagement which leads to outcomes. Those who read *Wired This Way* become more engaged. Now that we're engaged, let's collaborate, iterate and solve the problem.